Google Wor
Beginners Guide

A Practical Manual to Becoming a Pro in G. Suites
Productivity Apps for Easy Collaboration: Including
Gmail, Drive, Docs, Sheets, Slides, Chat, Meet, & More

Leslie J. Nemo

© Copyright 2023 Leslie J. Nemo. All rights reserved.

The content contained within this book may not be reproduced, duplicated or transmitted without direct written permission from the author or the publisher.

Under no circumstances will any blame or legal responsibility be held against the publisher, or author, for any damages, reparation, or monetary loss due to the information contained within this book. Either directly or indirectly. You are responsible for your own choices, actions, and results.

Legal Notice:
This book is copyright protected. This book is only for personal use. You cannot amend, distribute, sell, use, quote or paraphrase any part, or the content within this book, without the consent of the author or publisher.

Table of content

INTRODUCTION

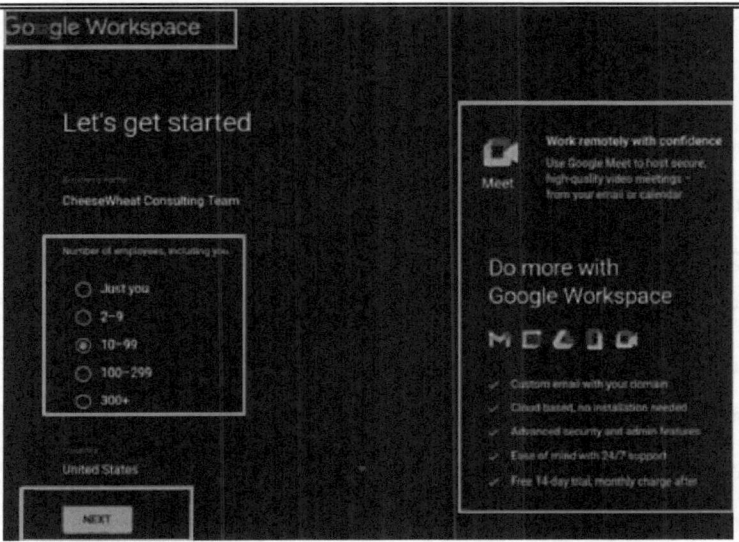

Google is way more than just a search engine. Its entire service list is nearly as astounding as the sheer volume of quick searches it performs in 24 hours—nearly one every millisecond. Additional services include word processing programs, spreadsheet operations, presentation creation, email reading, writing, and archiving, as well as appointment and meeting scheduling. Google has successfully integrated tools for collaboration, productivity, and communication directly into your web browser.

Google evolved from being merely a search engine to offering excellent services to its users. Even someone with exceptional proficiency in using these tools wouldn't be able to utilize them all at once, given the occasional craze for Google Applications. I believe that all users should stay up to date to be relevant in this rapidly evolving digital world.

Google Workspace is a collection of web applications and services hosted on Google's client computing infrastructure. Google Workspace comprises several applications such as Gmail, Google Drive online storage, Google Docs, Sheets, and Slides for productivity, Google Keep for taking notes, Google Forms for creating forms, sharing them, and receiving responses, and numerous chat apps like Google Meet and Google Chat.

Google is widely known for providing free services to people in exchange for part of their data. Users are not charged for using the Google search engine, Gmail email service, or Google Hangouts chat and video conference tool.

In contrast, Google Workspace is intended primarily for businesses and has a monthly fee for each user. If you work with Google goods, this is a terrific tool as it integrates all of the Google apps and makes them easier to use. I like how it brings together all of Google's features for collaboration and productivity into one easy-to-use package that several teams can use. The programs include Gmail, Hangouts, Calendar, Drive, Sites, Google Docs, Sheets, Forms, and Slides.

While many of the programs and services provided by Google Workspace are already freely available to and often used by individual clients, Google Workspace packages them into a comprehensive package that includes extra features and enhanced capabilities. Google Workspace, for example, offers additional storage on Google Drive, administrative tools for creating and managing user accounts, and the option for a company to use its domain for email addresses.

I use Google Workspace because it helps me organize and process data more quickly, which greatly simplifies my work and increases time efficiency. One thing I like is the ability to share and store files. This is so easy to use and intuitive that you don't need to be an expert to figure it out. It is highly engaging because sharing links and information with others is so simple.

As the go-to tool for all users in the modern world, Google offers much more than just search engines. We will be going over a few of the Google products and services in this book. This will introduce you to a plethora of Google-based opportunities that will help you with your daily tasks.

CHAPTER ONE

Starting Out

What Is Google Workspace?

Google Workspace is a collection of services and tools for cloud-based productivity and collaboration that it has created. Before being rebranded as Google Workspace in October 2020, it was known as G Suite. Google Workspace is a suite of tools and services intended to facilitate communication, teamwork, and productivity for both individuals and organizations.

Overview of Google Workspace Features

Among Google Workspace's essential components and features are the following:

1. **Gmail:** A well-known email provider that offers video conferencing, integrated chat, spam filtering, and business-class email addresses utilizing your domain name.

2. **Google Drive:** An online storage platform that facilitates the sharing and storing of data, documents, images, and videos. It also comes with online document creation and editing tools like Google Slides, Google Sheets, and

Google Docs for word processing and spreadsheets, respectively.

3. **Google Calendar**: This time-tracking and scheduling program lets users plan events, meetings, and appointments. It also lets users share their calendars with other people.

4. **Google Meet:** A video conferencing tool with built-in screen-sharing and chat capabilities that allows for online meetings, webinars, and video conferences.

5. **Google Chat:** This real-time messaging app facilitates group and direct talks as well as team collaboration. It is compatible with other Google Workspace applications.

6. **Google Forms:** A platform for making online quizzes, surveys, and forms for gathering and analyzing data.

7. **Google Sites:** This website builder facilitates the creation and publication of internal and external websites without the need for coding expertise.

8. **Google Keep:** An organizing and note-taking app for organizing and cataloging thoughts, lists, and reminders.

9. **Google Tasks:** An application for managing tasks and to-do lists that are linked with Google Calendar and Gmail.

10. **Admin Console:** An all-in-one management portal that lets administrators manage their Google Workspace

domain's security configurations, user access, and other features.

Importance Of Google Workspace

Google Workspace is a well-liked option for people, companies, and educational institutions due to its many advantages:

1. **Collaboration:** Google Workspace is made to facilitate teamwork. Collaboration across teams is facilitated by the real-time editing of documents, spreadsheets, and presentations by several people, irrespective of their geographical locations. Features like comments, discussion, and ideas improve teamwork even further.

2. **Cloud-based:** Since all of your data and files are kept online, you can access them from any location with an internet connection. This makes you more mobile and guarantees that you aren't dependent on any one gadget.

3. **Professional Email**: Google Workspace offers business email addresses that include your domain name, such as you@yourcompany.com. Moreover, it has features like personalized email routing, spam filtering, and sophisticated security settings.

4. **Integrated Apps:** A variety of integrated apps for email, document creation, calendar management, video conferencing, and other tasks are included in Google Workspace. The seamless integration of these apps will expedite your process.

5. **Scalability:** As your company expands or changes, adding or removing users is simple. Whether your company is a small startup or a large business, Google Workspace can grow to meet your demands.

6. **Security:** Two-factor authentication, frequent security upgrades, and data encryption are just a few of the strong security measures that Google Workspace provides. Google puts a lot of money into protecting your information.

7. **Reliability**: The uptime and dependability of Google's infrastructure are well-known. You can rely on your services to be there for you when you need them.

8. **Cost-Effective:** With its several subscription tiers, Google Workspace is accessible to companies of all sizes. It does away with the requirement for expensive on-premises maintenance and infrastructure.

9. **Mobile Compatibility:** You can continue to be productive while on the go thanks to Google Workspace apps' seamless mobile compatibility.

10. **Data Recovery and Backup**: Google offers solutions for data recovery and backups, lowering the possibility that information will be lost as a result of unintentional deletions or other problems.

11. **Collaborative Meetings:** Google Meet facilitates virtual meetings and high-quality video conferencing, which makes it simple to communicate with partners, clients, and team members anywhere in the world.

12. **Ease of Use:** New users will find Google Workspace's intuitive and user-friendly layout to be less of a learning curve.

13. **Third-Party Integration:** To improve its functionality and satisfy certain business needs, Google Workspace can be combined with a variety of third-party programs and services.

14. **Education-Focused Features**: Google Workspace for Education provides classroom management tools and collaboration capabilities, among other features, to educational institutions. These features are designed with educators' and students' requirements in mind.

Creating a Workspace account

Setting up a Google Workspace membership for your company or domain is necessary before creating an account. To create a Google Workspace account, follow these steps:

1. **Visit the Google Workspace Website:** Go to https://workspace.google.com/ to access the Google Workspace (previously G Suite) website. Select "Start Free Trial" or "Get started" from the menu.

2. **Select a Plan:** Venture Starter, Business Standard, Business Plus, Enterprise Essentials, Enterprise Standard, and Enterprise Plus are among the plans that Google Workspace provides. After deciding which plan best meets the needs of your company, click "Get started" under that option.

3. **Enter Your Domain:** Your domain name (yourcompany.com, for example) will need to be entered. If you don't already have one, you can utilize an already-registered domain that is with a domain registrar or register a new one with Google.

4. **Create a Google Account:** You must create a Google Account if you don't already have one linked to your domain. You can use this account to manage your

Google Workspace subscription as the administrator. Complete the form with your details and choose a strong password.

5. **Finish the Setup Process:** To finish the setup process, adhere to the on-screen instructions. To proceed, you must provide payment information if you aren't on a free trial, agree to the terms of service, and provide your contact details.

6. **Confirm Domain Ownership:** You must confirm domain ownership to use Google Workspace with your domain. Google will provide you instructions on how to add a DNS record or upload an HTML file to your website, which are the usual methods for confirming ownership.

7. **Set Up User Accounts:** You can begin setting up user accounts for your company once ownership has been confirmed. This includes creating email accounts (e.g., you@yourcompany.com) for your team members or employees. Depending on your needs, you can add users one at a time or in large quantities.

8. **Configure Settings and Customize**: After user accounts are created, you can set up security and access controls, alter Google Workspace's design with your

branding, and change settings. To manage these settings, use the Google Workspace Admin Console.

Navigating Google Workspace dashboard

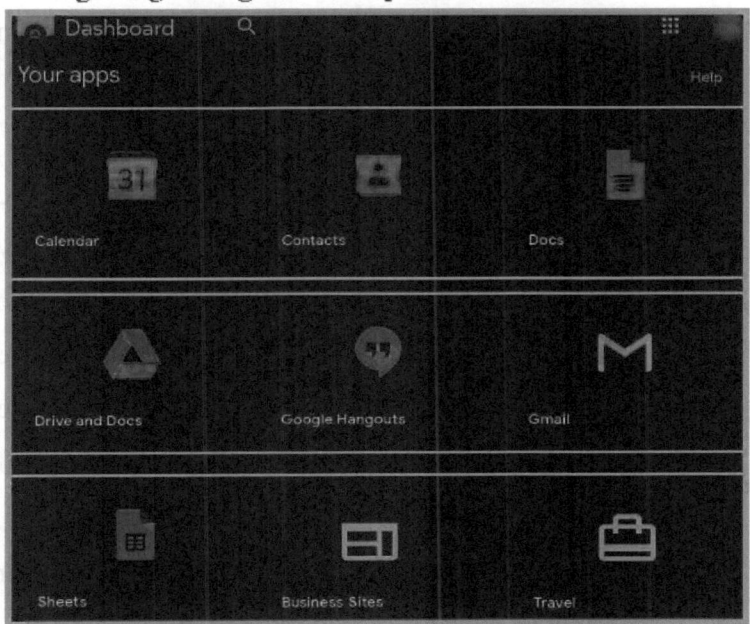

Using the Dashboard or App Launcher

There are two main ways to access and run the different apps and services offered by Google Workspace: the App Launcher (sometimes called the App Grid) and the Dashboard. Users can easily go to the tools and programs they want using these options. Here is how to apply each:

1. Dashboard:

You can add shortcuts to the Google Workspace services and apps that you use the most frequently to your Dashboard, a personalized homepage. The Dashboard's usage:

1. **Sign in to Google Workspace**: Enter your login information to access your Google Workspace account.

2. **Access the Dashboard**:
    *   When you sign in to the Google Workspace online interface, the Dashboard frequently appears as your homepage. Should that not be the case, you can obtain it by selecting the "Dashboard" option from the Google Workspace menu, which is typically found on the left side of the screen.
    *   If you have personalized your Dashboard, your selected shortcuts will be visibly displayed.

3. **Customize the Dashboard**:

    *   You can add or remove app and service shortcuts from the Dashboard to personalize it. Click the "+ Add shortcuts" button or the "Customize"

option, then choose the apps you wish to add to add a shortcut.

4. **Launch Apps**:

- The chosen program or service can be launched by clicking on the app shortcut.

2. App Launcher (App Grid):

App Launcher: The App Launcher, sometimes called App Grid, is a menu that looks like a grid and shows you all of the Google Workspace apps and services that you can use. For the App Launcher to work:

1. **Sign in to Google Workspace**: Enter your login information to access your Google Workspace account.

2. **Access the App Launcher**:

- Click the "App Launcher" icon to open the App Launcher. This indicator, which appears as a grid of squares or dots, is frequently found in the upper-right corner of the Google Workspace interface.
- As an alternative, you can launch the App Launcher by pressing the keyboard shortcut "Shift +." (Period).

3. **Navigate and Launch Apps**:

   - A grid of app icons can be seen in the App Launcher. To see the name of an app, hover your cursor over its icon; clicking the icon will start the program.

4. **Search for Apps**:

   - If you have a lot of apps, you can locate and open particular apps fast by using the search box at the top of the App Launcher. Just begin typing the name of the app, and the results of your search will show up.

Users can easily navigate and utilize the tools they require for productivity and collaboration with the help of the App Launcher and Dashboard, which are both designed to offer quick and simple access to the many Google Workspace apps and services. You can select the approach that best fits your workflow and preferences.

CHAPTER TWO

Introducing Gmail

Features of Gmail

Popular email provider Gmail provides several tools to make managing your emails easier. Here are a few of Gmail's salient characteristics:

1. **Search**: Gmail has an excellent search function that makes it simple and quick to locate particular emails. Emails can be found by keyword, sender, recipient, date, and other criteria.

2. **Labels:** You can arrange your emails using labels, which function similarly to folders. Labels can be made for various email categories and then applied to specific emails.

3. **Filters:** Filters let you automatically classify incoming emails into labels or groups according to predefined standards.

4. **Spam protection**: Gmail has a strong spam defense to assist in preventing unsolicited emails from entering your inbox.

5. **Undo send:** Gmail's "Undo send" function lets you take back an email that you unintentionally sent, and it does so in a matter of seconds.

6. **Keyboard shortcuts:** You can access your inbox and messages faster with the aid of several keyboard shortcuts available in Gmail.

7. **Snooze:** This function lets you hide an email from your inbox for a while and schedule its reappearance for a later time.

8. **Integration with other Google Workspace apps:** Gmail is a component of the Google Workspace productivity software family, which also consists of Google Sheets, Google Drive, and Google Docs.

Because of these characteristics, Gmail is a powerful and easy-to-use email service that can be used by a variety of users, including individuals, companies, and organizations, to help them manage their email correspondence more effectively.

Gmail Vs. Yahoo Mail

Two of the most widely used email services available right now are Gmail and Yahoo Mail. The following are some of the main variations between the two:

1. **Storage:** Yahoo Mail provides 1 TB of free storage, whilst Gmail provides 15 GB.

2. **Spam protection**: is a feature shared by Yahoo Mail and Gmail, while Gmail is widely thought to be better at weeding out unsolicited emails.

3. **Search:** Gmail offers an effective search function that makes it simple and quick to locate particular emails. Gmail has a more sophisticated search function than Yahoo Mail.

4. **User interface:** Gmail features an easy-to-navigate, clear, and intuitive user interface. The Yahoo Mail user interface can be more challenging to use and is more crowded.

5. **Integration with other apps**: Gmail is a component of the Google Workspace productivity app family, which also includes Google Sheets, Google Drive, and Google Docs. Not all apps are as well integrated with Yahoo Mail as they are.

6. **Mobile app**: You can access your email while on the road with the smartphone apps for Gmail and Yahoo Mail. On the other hand, most people agree that Gmail's mobile app is easier to use than Yahoo Mail's.

All things considered, Gmail and Yahoo Mail are both excellent email providers with a variety of tools to assist you in managing your correspondence. In the end, personal preference will determine which option you choose between the two.

How To set Up a Gmail Account

One particular kind of Google Account that is mainly utilized for email correspondence is a Gmail account. To put it simply, when you create a Gmail account, you are also creating a Google Account, complete with yourusername@gmail.com Gmail email address. In addition to allowing you to send and receive emails, this Gmail account gives you access to additional Google services.

You must first register for a Google account to create a Gmail address. You will be redirected to the Google account registration page by Gmail. Some basic details like your name, location, gender, and date of birth are required. Additionally, you'll need to give your new Gmail account a name. After making an account, you can begin customizing your mail settings and adding contacts.

To sign up for an account:

1. Visit www.gmail.com first.
2. Press Create account.

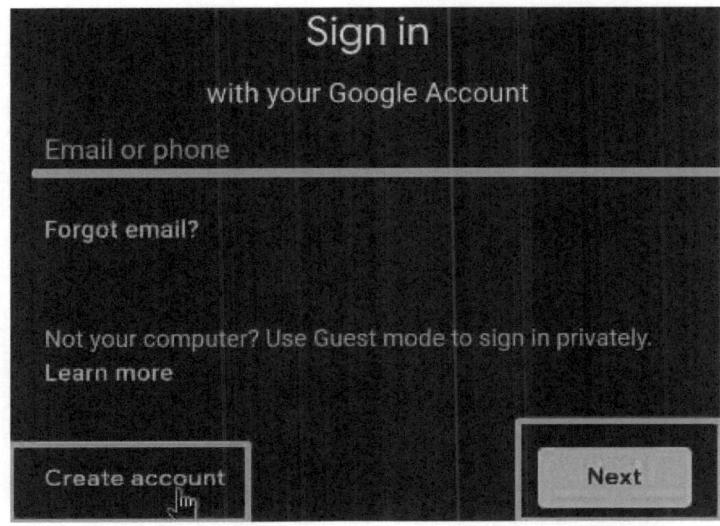

Sign in

with your Google Account

Email or phone

Forgot email?

Not your computer? Use Guest mode to sign in privately.
Learn more

Create account

Next

3. The registration form will show up. Fill in the necessary information as instructed.

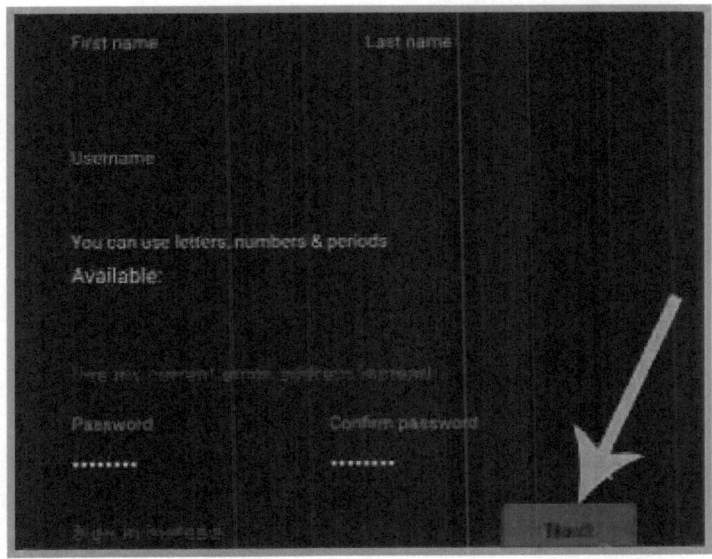

4. Next, enter your phone number to verify your account. Google uses a two-step verification process for your security.

5. Google will send you a text message including a verification code. To finish the account verification process, enter the code.

6. After that, a form requesting your data, such as your name and birthday, will appear.

7. Go over Google's privacy statement and terms of service, then choose "I agree."

8. A new account will be made for you.

Configuring Gmail Settings

You can optimize email management, improve security, and customize your email experience by configuring Gmail settings. The following is a step-by-step tutorial on setting up Gmail settings:

1. **Access your Gmail account and log in:**
   - Launch a web browser and navigate to https://mail.google.com/, the Gmail website.
   - Enter your email address and password to access your Gmail account.

2. **Navigate to the Menu Settings:**

- Click the gear symbol (⚙) next to your profile photo in the upper-right corner of the Gmail screen.

- Take note of the dropdown menu and choose "See all settings."

3. **General Settings:**

There are several tabs at the top of the Settings page. First, navigate to the "General" menu, which has the following crucial settings:

- **Language**: Modify the Gmail interface's language.

- **Vacation responder**: Configure an automated response for your absence.

- **Maximum page size**: Modify the quantity of talks on each page.

- **Stars:** Customize your stars and icons for marking emails.

- **Desktop notifications**: You can customize Gmail's desktop notifications to receive alerts when new emails arrive.

4. **Labels:**

You can manage your labels (folders) on the "Labels" tab by making new ones, renaming them, or hiding them.

5. **Inbox:**

You can set up your inbox type and Gmail's email classification system under the "Inbox" tab. "Default," "Important first," "Unread first," and other options are available.

6. **Accounts and Import:**

Using the "Accounts and Import" menu, you can:

- **Check mail from other accounts**: You can set up Gmail to retrieve emails from several accounts to check your mail from other accounts.
- **Send mail as**: Create and maintain email aliases.
- **Import mail and contacts**: Bring in contacts and emails from different accounts.

How to Compose and Send Emails

You can take the following actions in Gmail to write and send an email:

1. Log in to Gmail with the desired account.
2. Click **Compose** in the upper left corner.
3. Type the recipient's email address in the "To" column.
4. Provide a succinct email summary in the "Subject" field.

5. Type your message in the email's body.

6. Click the paperclip icon at the bottom of the window and choose the file you wish to attach if you want to attach one to your email.

7. Use the formatting choices located at the window's bottom to format your text.

8. Click **Send** to send your email when you're ready.

Replying to and Forwarding Emails

You can take the following actions to set up Gmail to reply to and forward emails:

1. Log in to Gmail using the desired account.

2. Click the gear icon in the upper right corner and choose **Settings**.

3. Select the **Forwarding and POP/IMAP** tab.

4. Select **Add a forwarding address** under the "Forwarding" column.

5. Click **Next** after entering the email address you wish to forward messages to.

6. Select **Proceed**, followed by **OK**.

7. That address will receive a verification mail. In that mail, click the verification link.

8. Reload your browser and return to the Gmail account's settings page from which you wish to forward messages.

9. In the "Forwarding" section, select **Forward a copy of incoming mail to**.

10. Decide what you want to do to the email copy that is stored in Gmail. We recommend **Keep Gmail's copy in the Inbox**.

11. Select **"Save Changes"** located at the bottom of the page.

Organizing Emails with Labels

You can take the following actions to use labels to arrange your Gmail inbox:

1. Log in to Gmail using the desired account.

2. Click the gear icon in the upper right corner and choose **Settings.**

3. Select the tab for **Labels.**

4. Click **Create new label** in the Labels area after swiping down.

5. Give your label a name, then select **Create.**

6. After choosing an email, click the **Label** icon at the top of the screen to apply a label to it.

7. From the list of possible labels, select the label you wish to apply to the email.

Managing Your Inbox

Archiving and Deleting Emails

In Gmail, you can take the following actions to archive or delete an email:

1. Log in to Gmail with the desired account.
2. Decide which email or emails you wish to archive or delete.
3. Select the **Archive** icon located at the top of the screen to archive the email or emails. You will find the email or emails in your "All Mail" folder.
4. Click the **Delete** icon at the top of the page to delete the email or emails. You will find the email or emails in your "Trash" folder.

Mark Emails as Read or Unread

You can take the following actions in Gmail to designate an email as read or unread:

1. Log in to Gmail with the desired account.

2. Choose the email or emails that you wish to label as read or unread.

3. Click the **"Mark as read"** button at the top of the screen to mark the email or emails as read. The chosen email or emails will be acknowledged as read.

4. Click the **"Mark as unread"** button at the top of the screen to designate the email or emails as unread. Email(s) that you have chosen will be tagged as unread.

Using Filters to Automatically Organize Emails

You can use these procedures to create filters that will automatically arrange your Gmail inbox:

1. Log in to Gmail using the desired account.

2. Click the gear icon in the upper right corner and choose **Settings**.

3. Select the tab labeled **Filters and Blocked Addresses**.

4. Select the **"Create a new filter"** option.

5. Fill in the corresponding fields with your filter criteria.

6. Select **"Create filter"**.

7. Select the desired label from the list of possible labels by checking the box next to **Apply the label.**

8. Opt for **"Create filter."**

Searching for Emails

Gmail's email search function is simple to use and intuitive. Here's how to use Gmail's email search function:

1. **Open Gmail:** To begin, go to your web browser and open your Gmail account. If you aren't already logged in, you will have to do so.

2. **Use the Search Bar:**

   - The Gmail interface's search bar is located at the top.
   - To open the search bar, click on it or just hit the "/" (forward slash) key on your keyboard.

3. **Enter Your Search Query:**

   - Type your search term into the search bar. To narrow down your search, you can include keywords, sender and recipient names, dates, subject lines, and more.
   - Gmail will make suggestions for search terms based on your input as you type, which helps facilitate finding what you're looking for.

4. **Click the search icon or hit Enter:**

   - To start the search after entering your search parameters, click the magnifying

glass-shaped search icon or hit Enter on
your keyboard.

5. **Examine Search Outcomes:**

- A list of emails that meet your search
  parameters will appear in Gmail. You can
  locate the desired email by swiping
  through the results.
- Gmail will make it simpler to find
  relevant emails by highlighting the search
  phrases within the email body.

Undo Send

The Undo Send function in Gmail can be useful if you sent
an email and discovered right away that it was incorrect.
With the help of this function, you can quickly retract an
email that you've sent. Use the following procedures to make
use of this feature:

1. Open Gmail on your PC.
2. Click the gear icon in the upper right corner and choose
   Settings.
3. Navigate to the area labeled **"Undo Send."**
4. Choose the desired **Send cancellation time** (5, 10, 20, or
   30 seconds).

5. Select **Save Changes** from the page's bottom menu.

Following the sending of an email, you will notice a notification in the lower left corner of your screen that reads "Message sent" and provides you with the choice to "View message" or "Undo." Clicking **"Undo"** will withdraw your email so you can edit it if needed before sending it again.

Keyboard Shortcuts

To turn on keyboard shortcuts in Gmail on a computer, follow these steps:

1. Access Gmail.
2. Click the gear icon in the upper right corner and choose **Settings.**
3. Navigate to the area labeled **"Keyboard shortcuts."**
4. Choose **Keyboard shortcuts on**.
5. Select **"Save Changes"** at the bottom of the page.

When Gmail is active, you can also get an exhaustive list of keyboard shortcuts by typing "?" Keep in mind that keyboard shortcuts on PCs and Macs operate differently.

Snooze Feature

With the help of the snooze feature, you can momentarily delete an email from your inbox and schedule its reappearance for a later time. If you want to deal with an email later but don't want it to take up space in your inbox right now, this can be helpful.

The procedures for using Gmail's snooze feature are as follows:

1. Launch Gmail.
2. Navigate to the email you wish to snooze.
3. Press the onscreen clock icon.
4. Select a time or day for the email to resurface in your inbox
5. Select **Snooze.**

Additionally, you can view snoozed emails by selecting **Snoozed** from the Gmail inbox's left-hand menu.

Collaborative Gmail Options

Sharing Files Through Gmail

It's simple to attach files to emails if you want to distribute files using Gmail. The steps to attach files to an email are as follows:

1. Launch Gmail.
2. Select **Compose** by clicking the button located in the upper left corner of your screen.
3. Select the paperclip symbol located at the bottom of the newly opened email window.
4. Choose the file or files to attach from Google Drive or your PC.
5. Select **"Open."**

Additionally, you have the option to drag & drop files straight from your PC into the email window.

Google Drive can be used as an alternative method of sharing files that are too big to attach to an email. To share a file using Google Drive, follow these steps:

1. Launch Google Drive first.
2. Upload the file you want to share.
3. To share a file, right-click on it and choose **Share.**

4. Type the recipient's email address in the sharing window to share the file with them.

5. Select if you want them to be able to read, write on, or edit the document.

6. Press **Send**.

An email containing a link to the file on Google Drive will be sent to the person you shared it with.

Accessing Gmail on Mobile Devices

You can get the Gmail app from the App Store or Google Play Store, depending on your mobile device, if you want to use Gmail on the go. The instructions to get the Gmail app are as follows:

1. On your mobile device, open the App Store or Google Play Store.

2. Type "Gmail" into the search field.

3. From the list of search results, choose the Gmail app.

4. To download and install the program, click Install or Get.

You can access your account and begin using Gmail on your mobile device after downloading and installing the Gmail app.

How to set up Gmail on your Mobile Devices

The following procedures can be used to set up Gmail on a mobile device:

1. Download the Gmail app from the App Store or Google Play Store, depending on your iOS or Android device.
2. Open the Gmail application.
3. Select **"Add account."**
4. Click on **Google.**
5. Click **Next** after entering your email address.
6. After entering your password, click **Next.**
7. Enter the verification code that was sent to your phone, if you have two-factor authentication enabled, and then click **Next.**
8. Click **I Agree** after reading the Terms of Service and Privacy Policy.
9. To create your account, adhere to the on-screen directions.

You can use Gmail on your mobile device after setting up your account.

CHAPTER THREE

Google Drive
Introduction To Google Drive

One of the most widely used cloud storage options accessible these days is Google Drive. Give the benefits of storing your files online some thought if you haven't used a cloud-based storage service like Google Drive before. Emailing or saving data to a USB drive is no longer necessary with Drive as files can be accessed from any computer with an Internet connection. Additionally, sharing files with others is made much simpler with Drive.

Google Drive is a free cloud-based file storage and retrieval service that lets you save files online and access them from any location. You can create documents, spreadsheets, presentations, and more with Google Drive's free web applications.

How to Set Up a Google Drive Account
Creating a Google Account

Setting up a Google account is simple. Some personal details, such as your name, age, and location, will be required.

You'll have easy access to additional Google services like Gmail, Google Docs, Google Calendar, and many more once you've successfully created and validated your account.

Not only does Gmail require a Google account to utilize, but it's simply one of the numerous services that Google offers to registered users. As a requirement of the sign-up process, you would also need to obtain a Gmail address. This implies that your Google account is automatically logged in every time you log into Gmail.

To register for a Google account, take these steps:

First, navigate to www.google.com.

Step 2: Click the Sign-in link in the page's upper-right corner.

Step 3: Tap Create an account.

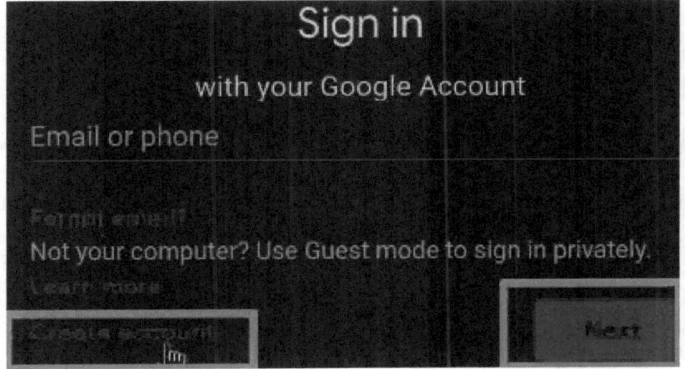

Step 4: The sign-up form will show up. After that, follow the instructions and enter the needed data.

Step 5: Enter your phone number.

Note: Your smartphone will receive an OTP (one-time password) from Google as a verification code. This would assist you in finishing the registration procedure.

Step 6: Choose Verify after entering the verification code that was texted to your phone.

Step 7: A page with personal information will show up. Enter your details, including your gender and date of birth, as instructed.

Step 8: Read Google's privacy statement and terms of service, then click "I agree."

Accessing Google Drive

You should be aware of how to access Google Drive files from any location if you frequently use devices other than your home computer or work remotely. You can access your files from any browser on any device once they have synchronized.

- How to use any web browser on any device to access Google Drive:
- Get any web browser installed.
- Go to Google Drive.

How to access Google Drive from a desktop computer:

- Install Google Drive for Mac/PC.
- On your desktop, open the Google Drive folder.

Note:

Unless you specify otherwise, the folder that you install using Google Drive will be saved in the default place on your computer.

The Google Drive Interface

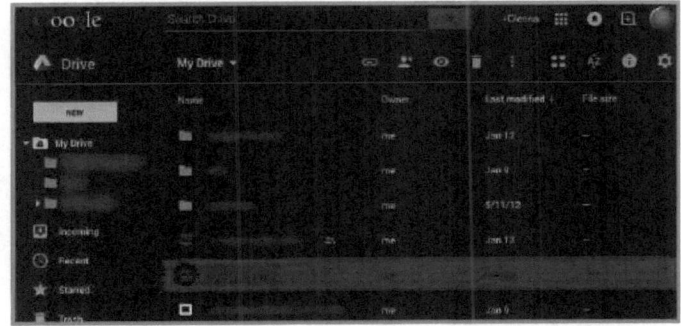

Google Drive for Mobile Devices

You can download the Google Drive app from the App Store or Google Play Store depending on your iOS or Android mobile device if you want to utilize Google Drive on the go. The instructions to get the Google Drive app are as follows:

1. On your mobile device, open the App Store or Google Play Store.
2. Type "Google Drive" into the search field.
3. From the search results, choose the Google Drive application.
4. To download and install the program, click Install or Get.

You can use Google Drive on your mobile device and sign into your account after downloading and installing the Google Drive app.

Google Drive for Desktop

You can use your web browser or the Google Drive app on a Mac or Windows computer to access Google Drive on a desktop computer. The instructions to get the Google Drive app are as follows:

1. Visit the Google Drive page.

2. Press the Download button located in the upper right corner of the LCD.

3. Choose "Personal Computer."

4. Select the desired version to download by clicking the Download button (Windows or Mac).

5. Then, install the program by following the directions on the screen.

Navigating The Google Drive Interface

Understanding the Main Components of the Google Drive Interface

The Google Drive interface is made up of multiple primary parts that let you organize and manage your files and folders. Here are a few of the essential elements:

1. **My Drive:** All of your files and folders are located in this primary drive. Your files can be shared with others and arranged into subfolders.

2. **Shared with me:** The files and folders in this folder were given to you by other people.

3. **Recent:** The files and folders that you have recently accessed or changed are displayed in this section.

4. **Starred:** The files and folders that you have starred or designated as important are displayed in this section.

5. **Trash:** The files and folders you have erased are displayed in this section. From here, you can either permanently remove them or restore them.

6. **Search bar:** You can look for particular files or folders using the search bar by using the file type, name, or keyword.

7. **File preview**: You can view a file on the Google Drive interface by clicking on it, and you don't even need to download it.

8. **Toolbar:** You can create new files, upload files, share files, and do a lot of other tasks with the toolbar at the top of the screen.

Customizing the Google Drive Interface

It is possible to alter the way your files and folders are shown on the Google Drive interface, in addition to the interface's color palette. Here are a few actions to get you going:

1. Launch Google Drive first.

2. In the upper right corner of the screen, click the **Settings** symbol.

3. Click on the drop-down menu and choose Settings.

4. You can customize the way your files and folders are shown by selecting the **General** tab. You have the option

to select the number of files displayed on each page in addition to selecting between a list view and a grid view.

5. You can adjust the amount of information that is shown for each file or folder in the **Display Density** section. You can choose between comfortable, cozy, and compact.

6. You can select the interface's color scheme in the **Theme** area. There are three options available: light, dark, and system default.

After making the necessary adjustments, click the **Done** button to save the configuration.

Creating and Uploading Files to Google Drive
MANAGING FILES IN GOOGLE DRIVE

Organizing Files with Folders and Subfolders

A great technique to keep your files and papers organized is to use folders and subfolders for file organization. Here are some actions to get you going:

1. Launch Google Drive first.

2. In the upper left corner of the screen, click the **New** button.

3. From the drop-down option, choose **Folder.**

4. After giving your folder a name, click **Create.**

5. Click on the folder you just created to open it and create a subfolder.

6. Press the New button once more, then choose Folder from the drop-down menu.

7. Click Create after giving your subdirectory a name.

To arrange your files, you can now drag & drop them into your folders and subfolders. To further organize your files, you can even make new subfolders inside of your existing subfolders.

Renaming and Deleting Files

The procedures below can be used to rename a file in Google Drive:

1. Launch Google Drive first.

2. To pick the file you wish to rename, click on it.

3. The More actions button, represented by three vertical dots, can be clicked in the upper right corner of the screen.

4. From the drop-down option, choose Rename.

5. Click OK after giving your file a new name.

To delete a file in Google Drive, follow these steps:

1. Launch Google Drive first.
2. To choose the file you wish to delete, click on it.
3. The trash can icon is located in the upper right corner of the screen. Click on it.
4. To verify that you wish to delete the file, click OK.

Moving and Copying Files

The steps below can be used to move a file within Google Drive:

1. Launch Google Drive first.
2. To pick the file you wish to move, click on it.
3. The More actions button, represented by three vertical dots, can be clicked in the upper right corner of the screen.
4. From the drop-down option, choose Move to.
5. Click Move after choosing the folder to which you wish to move the file.

Here's how to copy a file from Google Drive:

1. Launch Google Drive first.
2. To pick the file you wish to copy, click on it.

3. The More actions button, represented by three vertical dots, can be clicked in the upper right corner of the screen.

4. Decide From the drop-down menu, create a copy.

5. Choose the folder you wish to save the copied file in and give it a new name.

6. Press OK.

Sharing Files and Folders in Google Drive

Different Sharing Settings in Google Drive

There are various sharing options available in Google Drive that let you manage who can access, modify, or leave comments on your files and folders. The many sharing options in Google Drive are as follows:

1. **Private:** With this option, you can limit who can access your files and folders to only yourself.

2. **Anyone with the link:** This option enables access to your file or folder for anyone who has the link. They can see and edit the file without requiring a Google account.

3. **Anyone in your organization:** This option gives your file or folder access to anybody in your organization. To access or change the file, they need to be logged in and have a Google account.

4. **Public on the web:** This option makes your file or folder accessible to anybody with an internet connection. They can see and edit the file without requiring a Google account.

5. **Specific People:** You can share a file or folder with particular individuals by using this feature. You have the option to control who can read, write on, or alter the file.

Other sharing options that you can configure include whether users can share the file with other people if they require a password to open it, and if they must sign in using a Google account.

How to share Files and Folders in Google Drive
Use these procedures to share files and folders in Google Drive:

1. Launch Google Drive.
2. To pick the file or folder you wish to share, click on it.
3. Press the Sharing icon located in the upper right corner of the screen.
4. Type the recipient's email address in the sharing window to share the file or folder.
5. Make your choice about whether you want them to be allowed to open, view, or edit the folder or file.

6. Press Send.

Additionally, you can decide whether to send recipients an email when you share a file or folder with them.

Using Google Drive Offline
Enabling Offline Access to Google Drive

To allow Google Drive to be accessed offline, take the following actions:

1. Get Google Drive open.
2. In the upper right corner of the screen, click the Settings symbol.
3. From the drop-down box, choose Settings.
4. In the **Offline** tab, check the box next to **Sync Google Docs, Sheets, Slides & Drawings files to this computer so that you can edit offline**.
5. Press **"Done."**

You can access your Google Drive files and folders even when you're not online if you've enabled offline access. When you return to the internet, any modifications you make to your files will be immediately synchronized with your account.

Accessing Files and Folders Offline

You can set up Google Drive to allow offline access to files and folders by doing the following steps:

1. Open Google Drive.
2. In the upper right corner of the screen, click the Settings symbol.
3. From the drop-down box, choose Settings.
4. In the **Offline** tab, check the box next to **Sync Google Docs, Sheets, Slides & Drawings files to this computer so that you can edit offline**.
5. Press **"Done."**

You can access your Google Drive files and folders even when you're not online if you've enabled offline access. When you return to the internet, any modifications you make to your files will be immediately synchronized with your account.

Editing Files Offline

To allow offline access to Google Drive and modify files without an internet connection, take the following actions:

1. Open Google Drive.

2. In the upper right corner of the screen, click the Settings symbol.

3. From the drop-down box, choose Settings.

4. In the **Offline** tab, check the box next to **Sync Google Docs, Sheets, Slides & Drawings files to this computer so that you can edit offline**.

5. Press **"Done."**

You can access your Google Drive files and folders even when you're not online if you've enabled offline access. When you return to the internet, any modifications you make to your files will be immediately synchronized with your account.

Syncing Files Between Google Drive and your Computer

You can use the Google Drive desktop program to sync data between Google Drive and your PC. The steps to begin going are as follows:

1. Install the Google Drive desktop application on your PC after downloading it.

2. Open your Google account and log in.

3. Select the folders that you wish to sync between your computer and Google Drive.

4. Keep waiting for your computer to download the files.

Any modifications you make to your files after they've synchronized will be immediately synchronized with your Google Drive account.

Integrations with Other Google Workspace Apps

Google Drive on Mobile Devices
How to Use Your Phone to Upload Files to Google Drive

You can use the Google Drive app to upload files to Google Drive from your phone. The actions to take are as follows:

1. Install the Google Drive app from Google Play for Android devices or the App Store for iPhones and iPads.
2. Open your Google Account and log in.
3. Tap the plus symbol in the lower right corner of the app after opening it.
4. After choosing Upload, locate the files you wish to upload.
5. To confirm, tap Upload once again.

Sharing Files on Mobile Devices
You can use the Google Drive app to share files on mobile devices using Google Drive. The actions to take are as follows:

1. Install the Google Drive app from Google Play for Android devices or the App Store for iPhones and iPads.

2. Open your Google Account and log in.

3. Navigate to the file or folder you wish to share after opening the program.

4. From the upper right corner of the screen, tap the Share symbol.

5. Select the sharing method (such as email, messaging app, etc.) for the file or folder and adhere to the instructions.

Manage your Android Phone Backups

Android comes with a built-in cloud service that you can use to back up your phone. The actions to take are as follows:

1. Your Android device's Settings app should open.

2. Press System, followed by Backup.

3. Turn on the switch for **Back up to Google Drive**.

4. Click **Back up now** to see your backup settings.

Converting Files to PDF

Use Google Drive's built-in **"Save as PDF"** function to convert files to PDF format. The actions to take are as follows:

1. On your phone, launch the Google Drive app.
2. Locate the file you wish to convert, then press the button.
3. From the upper right corner of the screen, tap the three-dot icon.
4. From the list of options, choose Print.
5. Select Save as PDF from the printer list.
6. To confirm, tap Save.

Saving Files for Offline Access

Using the Google Drive app, you can store files for offline access. The actions to take are as follows:

1. On your phone, launch the Google Drive app.
2. Locate the file you wish to save, then press on it.
3. From the upper right corner of the screen, tap the three-dot icon.
4. Choose "Make available offline" from the drop-down menu.
5. At this point, the file can be accessed offline.

Please be aware that to access files offline, you must have a live internet connection. Furthermore, not every file type can be accessed offline. To provide offline access to a folder, you must enable offline access to each file within the folder.

Scanning Documents Using the Google Drive App

You can use the built-in Scan tool in the Google Drive app to scan documents. The actions to take are as follows:

1. On your phone, launch the Google Drive app.
2. From the lower right corner of the screen, tap the plus icon.
3. From the list of options, choose Scan.
4. After lining up your paper inside the frame, press the Shutter button.
5. If required, reposition the scan's corners, then hit Save to confirm.

To scan documents on your phone, you can also utilize third-party apps like CamScanner or Adobe Scan. You can download these apps for iOS and Android smartphones.

CHAPTER FOUR

Google Docs

Introduction

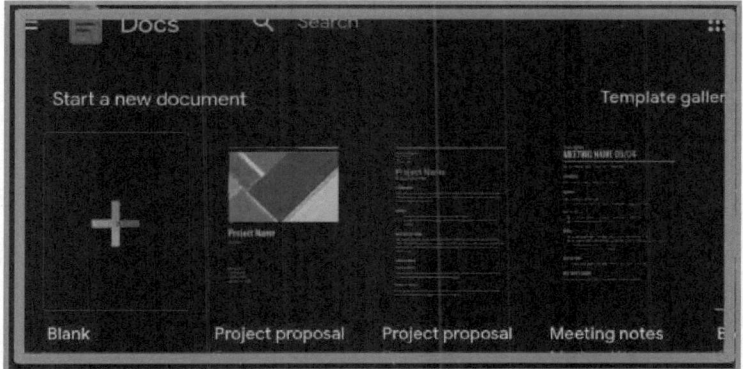

Google Docs is a word processor that runs in a browser. Online document creation, editing, and sharing are possible, and any computer with an internet connection can access it. Even a mobile app is available for iOS and android.

The collaborative capabilities of Google Docs are what distinguish it from Microsoft Word, its primary desktop rival. One of the earliest word processors that provide shared online document editing was Google Docs.

Google has greatly simplified the process of sharing documents between platforms and collaborating on them in real-time from a web browser window. Even without a

Google account, your colleagues can see and modify Google documents that you share with them.

Additionally, you can add missing features and increase functionality with Google Docs add-ons.

Setting Up Google Docs

Create a New Document

You can use the Google Docs app to start a new document in Google Docs. The actions to take are as follows:

1. Install the Google Docs app from Google Play for Android devices or the App Store for iPhones and iPads.
2. Open your Google Account and log in.
3. Tap the plus symbol in the lower right corner of the app after opening it.
4. Pick a Document from the drop-down menu.
5. Enter text into your document.

By following these instructions, you can also create a new document in Google Docs on your computer:

1. Open Google Docs.
2. Sign in to your Google Account.
3. Either choose Blank or choose a template to utilize as a foundation.

4. Enter text into your document.

Basic Formatting in Google Docs
How to Format Text and Paragraphs

You can utilize the formatting options found in the toolbar to format text and paragraphs in Google Docs. The following are a few of the most popular formatting choices:

1. **Bold:** Choose the text you wish to be bold, then press the keyboard shortcut Ctrl + B (Windows) or Cmd + B (Mac) to make it bold. You can also click the B icon in the toolbar.

2. **To make text italic**, select it and then click the I icon in the toolbar or use the keyboard shortcut Ctrl + I (Mac) or Ctrl + I (Windows).

3. **Underline:** Choose the text you wish to highlight, then click the U icon in the toolbar or press the Ctrl + U (Windows) or Cmd + U (Mac) keyboard shortcut.

4. **To strikethrough text**, select it and click the ABC icon in the toolbar. Alternatively, you can use the keyboard shortcut Alt + Shift + 5 on Windows or Option + Shift + 5 on Mac.

5. **Font:** To choose a different font, click the dropdown menu in the toolbar next to the font name.

6. **Font size:** To choose a different font size, click the dropdown menu in the toolbar next to the font size.

7. **Text color:** To change the text color, click the dropdown menu that appears next to the toolbar's text color icon.

8. **Highlight color:** To choose a different highlight color, click the dropdown menu next to the toolbar's highlight color symbol.

9. **Alignment:** To align your text left, center, right, or justify, click on one of the alignment buttons in the toolbar.

10. **Line spacing:** To choose a different line spacing, click the dropdown menu in the toolbar next to the line spacing.

For several of these formatting options, you can also use keyboard shortcuts. To set your text as Heading 1, for instance, use Ctrl + Alt + 1 (Windows) or Cmd + Option + 1 (Mac).

Adding Headers and Footers

You can use Google Docs' built-in Header & Footer functionality to add headers and footers. The actions to take are as follows:

1. On your phone, launch the Google Docs app.

2. From the lower right corner of the screen, tap the Edit (pencil) symbol.

3. Locate the page where you wish to add a header or footer by scrolling down.

4. From the upper left corner of the screen, tap the Insert menu.

5. Choose Header & Footer from the drop-down menu.

6. Select the Header or Footer choice from the drop-down menu.

7. Enter the text for your header or footer.

8. To confirm, tap Save.

Inserting Tables, Images, and Links

Using Google Docs, you can add tables, photos, and links by following these steps:

1. **Inserting Tables**: To insert a table, click its Table option from the toolbar and choose how many rows and columns to include. The table's border thickness, cell background color, and other elements can all be changed.

2. **Inserting Images**: Adding Images: From the toolbar, select the image you wish to insert by clicking on the Image option. An image from your PC or Google Drive can also be uploaded.

3. **Inserting Links:** Select the text that you wish to connect to by hovering over it and then selecting the connect toolbar option. After entering the URL you wish to link to, select Apply.

Using Styles and Themes

The following procedures can be used to utilize styles and themes in Google Docs:

1. **Using Styles:** To access a variety of pre-designed styles for your document, click the Styles option from the toolbar. There are numerous styles available for quotes, text, headers, and more. By altering the font, size, color, and other formatting parameters, you can further personalize the styles.

2. **Using Themes:** Choose Page setup from the File menu by clicking on it from the toolbar. You can choose from a variety of pre-made themes for your document by selecting the Themes option in the Page configuration dialog box. There are numerous themes to select from, each with its unique font pairings, color schemes, and backdrop pictures.

Creating and Using Templates

The following procedures can be used to create and utilize templates in Google Docs:

1. On your phone, launch the Google Docs app.
2. Open an already-existing document or start a new one.
3. Add the text, formatting, and images that you want to use in your template to personalize the document.
4. Choose Save as a template from the File menu that appears in the toolbar.
5. After giving your template a name, click Save.

You can take the following actions in Google Docs to use a template:

1. On your phone, launch the Google Docs app.
2. From the menu, select the Template Gallery option by clicking on it.
3. Look through the templates that are available or use keywords to find a particular one.
4. To utilize a template, click on it and choose Use this template.
5. After adding your content to the template, click Save.

Adding and Formatting Tables of Contents

Use Google Docs' Table of Contents function to add a table of contents. The actions to take are as follows:

1. Wherever you wish to insert the table of contents, place your cursor.
2. To pick the Table of contents, click the Insert menu located in the toolbar.
3. From the list of options, select a style for your table of contents.
4. The table of contents will be inserted into your document.

The following procedures can be used to format your table of contents:

1. To pick the table of contents, click on it.
2. Click on the **Paint format** icon from the toolbar.
3. Click on the heading or text that you wish to format.

Additionally, you can alter the font, size, color, and other formatting choices in your table of contents.

Advanced Features in Google Docs
GOOGLE DOCS ON MOBILE DEVICES

Accessing Google Docs on Mobile Devices

You can download and install the Google Docs app from Google Play for Android or the App Store for iPhone/iPad to access Google Docs on mobile devices. After installing the app, you can use your phone to create or edit documents by logging into your Google Account.

Editing and Collaborating on Documents on Mobile Devices

You can use the following procedures to edit and collaborate on projects in Google Docs on mobile devices:

1. On your phone, launch the Google Docs app.
2. Locate the document that you wish to modify or work together on.
3. To open the document, tap on it.
4. Start typing in the document to make changes, or modify the material that already exists.
5. Select the Share icon in the upper right corner of the screen and input the email addresses of the individuals you wish to share the document with to work with others.

6. Select if you want to allow them to view, modify, or comment on the document.

7. To share the document, tap Send.

On a PC, you can edit and collaborate on projects using Google Docs as well. Just sign in to your Google Account and navigate to Google Docs.

Tips And Tricks for Using Google Docs

Keyboard Shortcuts

You can follow these instructions to use keyboard shortcuts in Google Docs:

1. On your phone, launch the Google Docs app.

2. Open an already-existing document or start a new one.

3. Press Ctrl + / (Windows) or Cmd + / (Mac) to view a list of available keyboard shortcuts.

4. To accomplish a variety of tasks, including copying, pasting, undoing, redoing, and more, use the keyboard shortcuts.

The following are a few of the Google Docs keyboard shortcuts that are most frequently used:

- Cmd + C (Mac) or Ctrl + C (Windows): Copy

- Press Ctrl + V to paste (Windows) or Cmd + V (Mac).

- Cmd + X (Mac) or Ctrl + X (Windows): Cut
- Undo: Ctrl + Z (Mac) or Cmd + Z (Windows)
- Cmd + Y (Mac) or Ctrl + Y (Windows): Undo
- Mac users can use Cmd + B or Ctrl + B to bold text.
- Cmd + I (Mac) or Ctrl + I (Windows): Italic
- Cmd + U (Mac) or Ctrl + U (Windows): Underline
- Mac users can press Cmd + Option + 1 or Ctrl + Alt + 1 to access Heading 1.
- Macintosh: Cmd + Option + 2; Windows: Ctrl + Alt + 2; Heading 2
- Macintosh: Cmd + Option + 3; Windows: Ctrl + Alt + 3; Heading 3
  - To view an exhaustive list of keyboard shortcuts, simply hit Ctrl + / on Windows or Cmd + / on Mac.

Using Voice Typing

You can use the following procedures to enable voice typing in Google Docs:

1. On your phone, launch the Google Docs app.
2. Open an already-existing document or start a new one.
3. Place your cursor where you want to start typing.
4. Tap on the **Microphone** icon from the keyboard.
5. Get talking in a distinct and clear voice.

6. Your words will show on the screen as you talk.

7. Press the Microphone symbol once again to end voice typing.

Note that not all languages are supported via voice typing, and it might not function effectively in loud settings or with strong accents.

Using the Research Tool

You can take the following actions to use Google Docs' Research Tool:

1. On your phone, launch the Google Docs app.

2. Open an already-existing document or start a new one.

3. Select "**Explore**" from the Tools option that appears in the toolbar.

4. Enter your search term in the search field of the Explore panel that displays on the right side of the screen.

5. To begin your search, hit Enter or click the Search button.

6. You can see a list of search results that match your query in the Explore panel. To see additional details about any of the findings, simply click on it.

7. All you have to do is click and drag the link from the Explore panel into your document to include a link to a search result.

CHAPTER FIVE

Google Sheets
INTRODUCTION

With the web-based tool Google Sheets, users can create, edit, and modify spreadsheets as well as instantly share data online.

Features found in spreadsheets, such as adding, deleting, and sorting rows and columns, are available in Google's product. But in contrast to other spreadsheet apps, Google Sheets allows users who are spread out geographically to work together on a spreadsheet simultaneously and communicate via an integrated instant messaging app. Spreadsheets can be immediately uploaded by users from their PCs or mobile devices. Users can view other users' modifications as they are made, and the application instantly saves every modification.

One of the free online programs in the Google Docs Editors package is Google Sheets. Google Docs, Google Slides, Google Drawings, Google Forms, Google Sites, and Google Keep are also included in this package.

Collaborating on spreadsheets from different places is common with Google Sheets. A Google Sheets document can be edited in real-time by several users, with each user's modifications being recorded.

Users can create, edit, and format spreadsheets online for information organization and analysis with the Google Sheets spreadsheet application.

One or more sheets can be found in a Google spreadsheet. You can divide your spreadsheet into numerous sheets to better organize and facilitate finding information while working with a lot of data.

Setting Up Google Sheets
Accessing Google Sheets

Sheets can be opened using any of the following methods:

- Visit sheets.google.com using any web browser.
- Google Drive: Select New Google Sheets and start creating using a template or from scratch.
- The App Launcher Sheets can be clicked in the upper-right corner of most Google pages.
- On Android-powered devices, install and launch the application.
- Apple iOS devices: Download and launch the iOS application.

Creating a New Spreadsheet

You can use the Google Sheets app to create a new spreadsheet in Google Docs. The actions to take are as follows:

1. Install the Google Sheets app from Google Play for Android devices or the App Store for iPhones and iPads.
2. Open your Google Account and log in.
3. Tap the plus symbol in the lower right corner of the app after opening it.
4. Either select Blank or pick a template to get you started.
5. Begin inputting your information into the spreadsheet.

On a computer, you can also make a new spreadsheet in Google Sheets by doing the following steps:

1. Go to Google Sheets.
2. Open your Google Account and log in.
3. Either choose Blank or choose a template to utilize as a foundation.
4. Begin inputting your information into the spreadsheet.

Basic Functions of Google Sheets

Adding and Editing Data

You can take the following actions to add data to a Google Sheets spreadsheet:

1. On your phone, launch the Google Sheets app.
2. Locate the spreadsheet you wish to modify, then tap to open it.
3. Wherever you wish to add data, tap in that cell.
4. Input your data into the cell by typing it in.
5. Just tap on the cell and make your edits to the existing data.

In addition, you can add or modify data in numerous cells at once by using the Copy and Paste commands. Just choose the cells you wish to copy, press the Copy icon in the toolbar, choose the destination cells, and then tap the Paste icon to accomplish this.

Tips for Efficient Data Entry

Here are some pointers for productive Google Sheets data entry:

1. Keyboard shortcuts can help you work more quickly. As an illustration, you can copy data using Ctrl + C

(Windows) or Cmd + C (Mac) and paste data using Ctrl + V (Windows) or Cmd + V (Mac).

2. To swiftly fill up a set of cells with a pattern, use the AutoFill function. To finish a series, you can drag the fill handle after typing the first few numbers in the sequence.

3. To make sure that data is entered accurately, use the Data Validation tool. One possible use for this would be to create a validation rule that restricts the number of entries in a given cell to those between 1 and 100.

4. To draw attention to cells that satisfy specific requirements, use the Conditional Formatting function. Conditional formatting can be used, for instance, to highlight all cells that contain a specific word or phrase.

5. To quickly create charts and graphs based on your data, use the Explore function. To visualize the data, just pick it and click the Explore icon in the toolbar.

6. Sort and filter your data easily by using the Filter function. You can use filters, for instance, to sort your data according to a certain column or display just rows that match certain requirements.

Formatting Cells

The following procedures can be used to format cells in Google Sheets:

1. You can format the cells by selecting them.
2. From the toolbar, click the Format option and choose Number or Align.
3. From the list of possibilities, select a formatting option.
4. The chosen cells will receive the formatting.

The following are a few of the most popular formatting choices:

- **Number:** This option allows you to format cells as dates, times, percentages, currencies, and more.
- **Align:** This feature allows you to center text within a cell either vertically or horizontally.

Additionally, you can utilize conditional formatting to highlight cells that satisfy specific requirements. Conditional formatting can be used, for instance, to highlight all cells that contain a specific word or phrase.

Using Basic Formulas and Functions

You can wish to start with the fundamental formulas and functions in Google Sheets if you're new to using them. Cell formulas, which are often present in most desktop spreadsheet programs, are supported by Google Sheets. Formulas that handle data and compute strings and integers can be built using functions. The complete list of functions available in each category is provided below:

- **Date**: DATE, DATEDIF, DATEVALUE, DAY, DAYS, DAYS360, EDATE, EOMONTH, EPOCHTODATE, HOUR, ISOWEEKNUM, MINUTE, MONTH, NETWORKDAYS, NETWORKDAYS.INTL, NOW, SECOND, TIME, TIMEVALUE, TODAY, WEEKDAY.

You have the option to choose between 21 other languages and English when using Google Sheets.

Advanced Features in Google Sheets

Conditional Formatting

Here's a quick tutorial on using Google Sheets' conditional formatting:

1. Launch the Google Sheets file that needs formatting.
2. Choose which cells to apply format rules to.

3. Pick Conditional formatting under Format. It will reveal a toolbar on the right.
4. To create a rule, go to "Format cells if" and choose the condition that you wish to apply to the rule.
5. Select the "Formatting style" that describes how the cell will appear when certain circumstances are met.
6. Press "Done."

Additionally, you can apply formatting to one or more cells dependent on the contents of other cells by using custom formulas with conditional formatting. You can, for instance, highlight test results to identify pupils who received less than 80%.

Data Validation

Google Sheets has a tool called data validation that lets you restrict the kind of information users can submit in particular cells. Data validation can be used to reject faulty data completely or to warn the user when they enter invalid data 1.

The steps to apply data validation in Google Sheets are as follows:

1. Launch the Google Sheets file that needs formatting.

2. Choose which cells to apply format rules to.

3. Select Data > Data Validation. It will reveal a toolbar on the right.

4. Choose the circumstance under "Criteria" that you wish to apply to the rule to create it.

5. Select the appearance of the cell under "Appearance" when certain circumstances are met.

6. Press Save.

Additionally, you can apply formatting to one or more cells dependent on the contents of other cells by using custom formulas with conditional formatting. You can, for instance, highlight test results to identify pupils who received less than 80%.

Pivot Tables and Charts

The following is a quick tutorial on using charts and pivot tables in Google Sheets:

1. Launch the Google Sheets file that needs formatting.

2. Decide which data range you wish to use to build a pivot table.

3. Select Pivot Table under Data. It will reveal a toolbar on the right.

4. Click on the "Rows" area and choose the column you wish to combine.
5. Please choose the column you wish to summarize from the "Values" section.
6. Select "Create."

Based on your pivot tables, you can also make pivot charts. They are as follows:

1. The pivot table for which you wish to make a chart should be clicked.
2. From the toolbar above the sheet, select Insert chart.
3. Select the desired chart type and make any necessary adjustments.
4. Click Insert.

Macros and Scripts

The following is a quick tutorial on using scripts and macros in Google Sheets:

1. Launch the Google Sheets file that needs formatting.
2. Select Script editor under Tools. It will open in a new tab.
3. Write your script in the editor.
4. To save the script, select **File > Save**.

5. Snap out of the script editor tab.

6. Refresh your Google Sheets document.

7. To run your macro, select Tools > Macros > Your Macro Name.

8. You can also use pre-built macros from the Google Sheets add-ons store. These add-ons can help you automate tasks such as sending emails, generating reports, and more.

Integrations With Other Google Workspace Apps

Using Google Sheets with Google Drive

The following is a quick tutorial on utilizing Google Sheets with Google Drive:

1. Open Google Drive.

2. To start a new spreadsheet, select **New > Google Sheets.**

3. Click New > File upload to upload an existing spreadsheet as well.

4. A spreadsheet that you have developed or uploaded can be accessed via Google Drive.

5. Click the Share button located in the upper right corner of the screen to distribute the spreadsheet to other people.

6. By selecting File > Download, you can also download the spreadsheet in several different formats.

Importing and Exporting Files to Microsoft Excel and Other Formats

Here's a quick tutorial on using Google Sheets to import and export files to Microsoft Excel and other formats:

1. To export a Google Sheets document, open it.

2. To download the file in Excel format, select File > Download > Microsoft Excel (.xlsx).

3. By selecting File > Download, you can also download the file in additional formats including CSV, PDF, and HTML.

4. Click File > Import > Upload and choose the Excel file you wish to import into Google Sheets.

5. By selecting File > Import, you can also import files in various formats, like CSV, TSV, and ODS.

Google Sheets on Mobile Devices

Accessing Google Sheets on Mobile Devices

Here's a quick tutorial on using Google Sheets on a mobile device:

1. Get the Google Sheets app from the Google Play Store (Android) or App Store (iOS).

2. Sign in to your Google account after opening the app.

3. By tapping the plus icon in the lower right corner of the screen, you can start a new spreadsheet.

4. Select Open from the menu icon located in the upper left corner of the screen to access an already-existing spreadsheet.

5. You can also click Share from the menu icon to share your spreadsheet with other people.

Editing Spreadsheets on Mobile Devices

Here's a quick tutorial on using mobile devices to edit spreadsheets:

1. Get the Google Sheets app from the Google Play Store (Android) or App Store (iOS).

2. Sign in to your Google account after opening the app.

3. Click the plus symbol in the lower right corner of the screen to start a new spreadsheet.

4. Select Open from the menu icon located in the upper left corner of the screen to access an already-existing spreadsheet.

5. You just need to tap on a cell and begin typing to edit it.

6. Tap the Plus icon above or to the left of the cell, you wish to add a new row or column to.

7. Tap and hold the row or column header, then choose Delete to remove the row or column.

8. Choose the cells you wish to format, then pick Format from the toolbar above the sheet.

CHAPTER SIX

Google Slides
Introduction

One of the Google Docs suite's applications is a presentation graphics program. Google Slides is a presentation tool that works in the browser, much like Microsoft's long-standing PowerPoint product.

It has almost all of the features included in a conventional presenting program, like Microsoft PowerPoint. With cloud storage provided by Google Slides, customers' work is automatically saved and can be recovered if their SSD or hard drive dies.

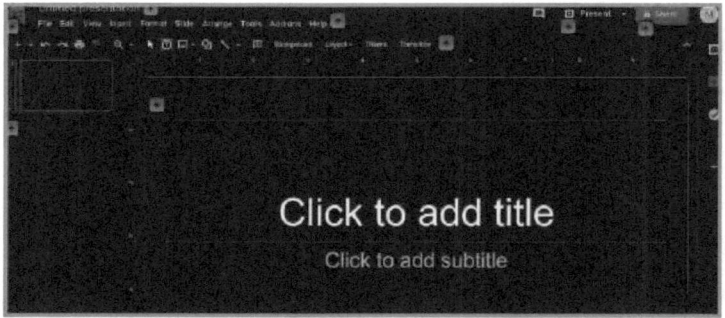

Setting Up Google Slides
Here is a brief guide on how to set up Google Slides:

1. Get Google Drive open.

2. Create a new presentation by selecting New > Google Slides.

3. To upload an already-made presentation, select New > File upload.

4. A presentation that you have made or uploaded can be accessed via Google Drive.

5. Click the Share button located in the upper right corner of the screen to share the presentation with others.

6. By selecting File > Download, you can also download the presentation in several different formats.

Accessing Google Slides

Go to slides.google.com to access the Slides home screen. Under "Start a new presentation," in the upper left corner, select New. This will launch and generate a new presentation for you.

Creating a New Presentation

To create a new presentation:

1. Go to slides.google.com to access the Slides home screen.

2. Under "Start a new presentation," in the upper left corner, select New Plus. This will launch and generate a new presentation for you.

Additionally, you can make new presentations by visiting https://slides.google.com/create.

Basic Functions of Google Slides

Adding and Editing Slides

The following is a quick tutorial on adding and editing slides in Google Slides:

1. To update a Google Slides document, open it.
2. Use Ctrl + M or select Insert > New slide to add a new slide. To duplicate an already-existing slide, you can also right-click on it and choose Make a copy.
3. To remove a slide, simply perform right-click on the desired slide and choose Delete slide.
4. Click Slide > Change layout and choose the desired layout to alter the arrangement of a slide.
5. Click the text box and begin typing to add text to a slide.
6. To incorporate a picture into a PowerPoint, choose the desired image by clicking Insert > picture.
7. Use the toolbar above the slide to format text or pictures.

Formatting Text and Images

Here is a brief guide on how to format text and images in Google Slides:

1. To update a Google Slides document, open it.
2. To format text, choose the text to be formatted and make changes to the font, size, color, and other aspects using the toolbar above the slide.
3. To include an image, choose the desired image by clicking Insert > Image. The image can then be adjusted, cropped, and resized using the toolbar above the presentation.
4. To incorporate a shape, choose the desired shape by clicking Insert > Shape. Then, you can alter the border and fill colors, among other things, using the toolbar that is above the slide.
5. You can draw a line or an arrow on the slide by selecting Insert > Line or Arrow and then drawing the line or arrow. The line color, thickness, and other properties can then be adjusted using the toolbar located above the slide.

Using Themes and Templates

The following is a quick tutorial on using Google Slides themes and templates:

1. Launch the Google Slides file that needs formatting.
2. To select a different theme for your presentation, select Slide > Change theme.
3. To apply a theme customization, select Slide > Edit master and edit the master slide.
4. Click File > New > From template and choose the template you wish to use to apply it to your presentation.
5. By selecting File > Make a copy of an existing presentation and editing the copy, you can also make your unique templates.

Advanced Features in Google Slides

Integrations With Other Google Workspace Apps

Using Google Slides with Google Drive

Here's a quick tutorial on using Google Drive with Google Slides:

1. Get Google Drive open.
2. Create a new presentation by selecting New > Google Slides.

3. To upload an already-made presentation, select New > File upload.

4. A presentation that you have made or uploaded can be accessed via Google Drive.

5. Click the Share button located in the upper right corner of the screen to share the presentation with others.

6. By selecting File > Download, you can also download the presentation in several different formats.

Importing and Exporting Files to Microsoft PowerPoint and Other Formats

Here's a quick tutorial on using Google Slides to import and export files to Microsoft PowerPoint and other formats:

1. To export a Google Slides document, open it.

2. To download the file in PowerPoint format, select File > Download > Microsoft PowerPoint (.pptx).

3. By selecting File > Download, you can also download the file in additional formats like PDF, JPEG, and SVG.

4. To import a PowerPoint file into Google Slides, choose the desired file by clicking File > Import > Upload.

5. By selecting File > Import, you can also import files in various formats, including PDF, JPEG, and SVG.

Google Slides on Mobile Devices

Accessing Google Slides on Mobile Devices

This is a quick tutorial explaining how to use Google Slides on a mobile device:

1. From the Google Play Store (Android) or App Store (iOS), download the Google Slides app.
2. Sign in to your Google account after opening the app.
3. Click the plus symbol in the lower right corner of the screen to start a new presentation.
4. Click the menu button in the upper left corner of the screen, then choose Open to start an already-open presentation.
5. Moreover, you can pick Share from the menu button and share your presentation with other people.

Creating New Google Slides on Mobile Devices

Here's a quick tutorial on using mobile devices to create new Google Slides:

1. From the Google Play Store (Android) or App Store (iOS), download the Google Slides app.
2. Sign in to your Google account after opening the app.

3. Click the plus symbol in the lower right corner of the screen to start a new presentation.

4. You can type content into the text boxes to add a title and subtitle to your presentation.

5. Click the + symbol in the lower-left corner of the screen to add a new slide.

6. By selecting Layouts from the toolbar above the presentation, you can select from several different slide layouts.

7. Simply tap the text box and begin typing to add text to a slide.

8. Select the desired image by tapping Insert > Image and adding it to a slide.

9. Use the toolbar above the slide to format text or pictures.

Editing and Collaborating on Presentations on Mobile Devices

Here's a quick tutorial on using mobile devices to modify and collaborate on presentations:

1. From the Google Play Store (Android) or App Store (iOS), download the Google Slides app.

2. Sign in to your Google account after opening the app.

3. Click the plus symbol in the lower right corner of the screen to start a new presentation.

4. Click the menu button in the upper left corner of the screen, then choose Open to start an already-open presentation.

5. Just tap on a slide and begin typing to alter it.

6. Click the + symbol in the lower-left corner of the screen to add a new slide.

7. Swipe left on the slide you wish to remove, then press Delete.

8. Use the toolbar above the slide to format text or pictures.

9. You can invite other people to edit your presentation by tapping the Share icon located in the upper right corner of the screen.

CHAPTER SEVEN

Google Meet

Introduction

Google has created a video conferencing application called Google Meet. Up to 250 people can participate in and host video meetings using this feature. Both an iOS and Android mobile app and a web version of Google Meet are accessible. It has capabilities including the capacity to record meetings, real-time captioning, and screen sharing. It is simple to arrange and join meetings straight from Google Meet by integrating it with other Google Workspace products like Gmail and Google Calendar.

Setting Up Google Meet

Accessing Google Meet

Take these actions to gain access to Google Meet:

1. Launch your browser, then navigate to meet.google.com.
2. To join or begin a meeting, click.
3. Enter the code or nickname for the meeting that was given to you by the host.
4. Select "Join."

Alternatively, simply clicking on the meeting link included in the email or event invitation, you can join a meeting straight from Gmail or Google Calendar.

Scheduling a Meeting

The steps below can be used to set up a meeting in Google Meet:

1. Launch the Google Calendar.
2. To add a new event, click the Create button.
3. Add information about the event, including the date, time, and title.
4. To add a video conference connection to the event, click on Add Google Meet video conferencing.
5. To save the event, click Save.

By clicking on the video conferencing link in the event invitation, guests can now join the conference if you have shared it with them.

Inviting Participants

You can use these procedures to invite people to a Google Meet meeting:

1. Launch the Google Calendar.

2. Select the event you wish to send out invitations for.

3. To make changes to the event, click the Edit button.

4. Enter the email addresses of the individuals you wish to invite to the Guests area.

5. To save the changes, click Save.

As an alternative, you can copy the meeting link and send it to attendees through instant messaging services or emails.

Basic Functions of Google Meet

Joining a Meeting

You can join a Google Meet meeting by doing the following:

1. Launch your browser, then navigate to meet.google.com.

2. To join or begin a meeting, click.

3. Enter the code or nickname for the meeting that was given to you by the host.

4. Select "Join."

Alternatively, by clicking on the meeting link included in the event invitation, you can join a meeting straight from Gmail or Google Calendar.

Adjusting Audio and Video Settings

To adjust your audio and video settings in **Google Meet**, follow these steps:

1. Launch the Google Meet meeting.
2. In the lower right corner of the screen, click the Settings symbol.
3. For each, click to change the settings by clicking on Audio or Video.
4. You can select your speaker and microphone, change the level, and test your audio in the Audio options.
5. You can select your camera and change the video quality in the Video options.
6. After making the necessary adjustments, click Save to keep the configurations.

You can now have a better Google Meet meeting experience with audio and video.

Using Chat and Reactions

During a meeting, attendees can text each other using Google Meet's chat feature. Click the conversation icon at the bottom of the screen to utilize the conversation feature. The message can then be typed and sent to each member of the meeting or a single person.

Furthermore, Google Meet has a response function that lets users respond to what is being said without disturbing the speaker. Click the Reactions icon at the bottom of the screen to access the reactions function. Then, you have a selection of responses to choose from, like heart, laughter, thumbs up, and more.

Collaboration in Google Meet

Screen Sharing

Use these steps to share your screen in Google Meet:

1. Launch the Google Meet meeting.
2. In the lower right corner of the screen, click the Present Now button.
3. Decide what you wish to disclose. You have the option to share a window, a Chrome tab, or your whole screen.
4. To begin sharing your screen, click Share.

During your Google Meet meetings, you can now share your screen with other participants.

Advanced Features in Google Meet
SECURITY AND PRIVACY IN GOOGLE MEET

Controlling Access to Meetings

Take the following actions to manage who can access a Google Meet meeting:

1. Launch the Google Meet meeting.
2. In the lower right corner of the screen, click the People symbol.
3. To let people join the meeting, click Admit; to keep them from joining, click Deny.
4. Click on the Lock meeting button in the lower left corner of the screen to stop participants from joining after they have been removed.

You can now manage who can join meetings held with Google Meet.

Enabling Waiting Rooms and End-to-End Encryption

To enable waiting rooms in **Google Meet**, follow these steps:

1. Launch the Google Meet meeting.
2. In the lower right corner of the screen, click the Settings symbol.

3. Turn on the waiting area.

4. To save the changes, click Save.

To activate end-to-end encryption in Google Meet, take the following actions:

1. Launch the Google Meet meeting.

2. In the lower right corner of the screen, click the Settings symbol.

3. Turn on encryption from end to end.

4. To save the changes, click Save.

You can now utilize end-to-end encryption and waiting areas during Google Meet meetings.

Integrations With Other Google Workspace Apps

Using Google Meet with Google Calendar and Gmail

Google Meet facilitates the scheduling and joining of meetings directly from other Google Workspace applications, like Gmail and Google Calendar.

The steps below can be used to set up a meeting in Google Meet:

1. Launch the Google Calendar.

2. To add a new event, click the Create button.

3. Add information about the event, including the date, time, and title.

4. To add a video conference connection to the event, click on Add Google Meet video conferencing.

5. To save the event, click Save.

You can use these procedures to invite people to a Google Meet meeting:

1. Launch the Google Calendar.

2. Select the event you wish to send out invitations for.

3. To make changes to the event, click the Edit button.

4. Enter the email addresses of the individuals you wish to invite to the Guests area.

5. To save the changes, click Save.

You can join a Google Meet meeting by doing the following:

1. Launch your browser, then navigate to meet.google.com.

2. To join or begin a meeting, click.

3. Enter the code or nickname for the meeting that was given to you by the host.

4. Select "Join."

In Google Meet, click the Settings icon in the lower right corner of the screen, then select Audio or Video to change your audio and video preferences.

Google Meet can now be used with other Google Workspace applications, such as Gmail and Google Calendar.

Google Meet on Mobile Devices

Accessing Google Meet on Mobile Devices

Use these methods to access Google Meet on a mobile device:

1. Get the Google Meet app from the Google Play Store (Android) or App Store (iOS).
2. Sign in to your Google account after opening the app.
3. You can input the meeting code or nickname or tap on the meeting link that the meeting organizer has supplied.
4. To join the meeting, tap Join.

Alternatively, by tapping the meeting link included in the event invitation, you can join a meeting straight from Gmail or Google Calendar.

Joining and Hosting Meetings on Mobile Devices

Use Google Meet on your mobile device to join or host meetings by following these steps:

1. Get the Google Meet app from the Google Play Store (Android) or App Store (iOS).
2. Sign in to your Google account after opening the app.
3. You can enter the meeting code or username, or touch the meeting link that the meeting organizer has provided, to join the meeting.
4. Click New Meeting, then select Start an instant meeting to start a meeting as the host.
5. Select whether to activate your microphone and camera.
6. Press the Join or Start meeting buttons.

Google Meet now allows you to host or attend meetings on mobile devices.

Troubleshooting Common Issues in Google Meet

Audio and Video Problems

If you're having issues with Google Meet's audio or video, try these troubleshooting steps:

1. Verify that you have a steady internet connection and that you have enough bandwidth to use for video conferences.

2. Verify the settings on your device to ensure that the microphone and camera are turned on and are not being utilized by another app.

3. Restart your device: Restarting your device might occasionally help fix issues with audio and video.

4. Clear the cache in your browser: This can help fix problems with video conferencing.

5. Update your browser: Verify that the web browser version you are using is the most recent one.

6. Try a different web browser: If the issues persist, consider switching to a new browser.

7. Contact support: For additional help, get in touch with Google Meet support if none of the aforementioned solutions work.

Connection Issues

You can troubleshoot the issue by following these steps:

1. Verify that you have a steady internet connection and that you have enough bandwidth to use for video conferences.

2. Verify the settings on your device to ensure that the microphone and camera are turned on and are not being utilized by another app.

3. Restart your device: Restarting your device might occasionally help fix issues with audio and video.

4. Clear the cache in your browser: This can help fix problems with video conferencing.

5. Update your browser: Verify that the web browser version you are using is the most recent one.

6. Try a different web browser: If the issues persist, consider switching to a new browser.

7. Contact support: For additional help, get in touch with Google Meet support if none of the aforementioned solutions work.

Settings and Permissions

Take these actions to get to Google Meet's settings and permissions:

1. Launch the Google Meet meeting.

2. In the lower right corner of the screen, click the Settings symbol.

3. Select the permissions or settings that you wish to change.

You can change a lot of settings, including screen sharing, audio and video quality, and more. Permissions like who can join the meeting, share their screen, and more can also be changed.

CHAPTER EIGHT

Google Forms
Introduction

With the free web tool Google Forms, you can make quizzes, surveys, and other types of content. It is a component of the Google suite of web applications, which also includes Google Slides, Google Sheets, and Google Docs. It's a flexible tool that can be used for many different tasks, such as making a pop quiz or collecting RSVPs for an event.

To create a Google Form, you'll need a Google account; however, you can change the settings to make the form accessible to everyone, negating the requirement for a Google account.

Setting Up Google Forms
Accessing Google Forms

Step 1: Create a brand-new survey or test. Open the forms.google.com page.

Step 2: Format and edit a survey or workbook. Text, photos, and videos can all be added, edited, or formatted in a form.

..

Step 3: Forward your form to recipients for completion. When you're ready, you can distribute your form to people and get their answers.

Creating a New Form

The Google Forms app is the easiest place to start when developing a form.

After logging into your Google account, go to the Google Forms website.

Sign in with your Google account if asked.

Pick Proceed to Forms.

Choose Blank from the "Start a new form" menu.

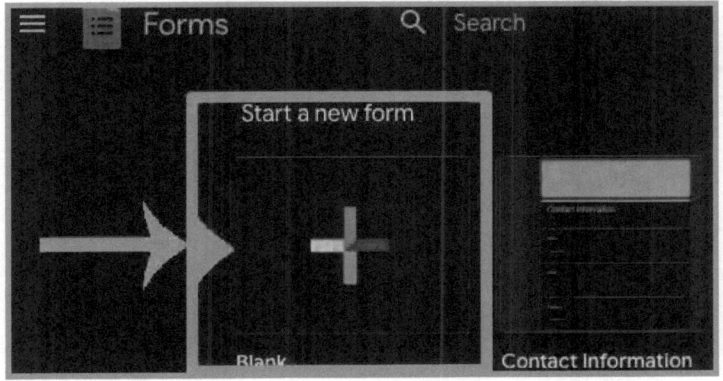

For your form (A), provide a title and an optional description.

For the first question (B), type text.

Under the drop-down menu (C), choose the input type you wish to receive.

Provide options for responses if appropriate (D).

Click the Plus button (E) on the right side of the screen to add more questions.

Click the Send button located in the upper-right corner of the form once it is finished.

Basic Functions of Google Forms

Adding and Editing Questions

Use these procedures to create and modify questions in Google Forms:

1. Go to Google Forms and open the form.
2. To add a new question, click the Add button.
3. From the list of options, select the kind of question you wish to add.
4. Type the potential answers to your query.
5. Turn on Required to stop individuals from not responding.

1. Click on the question or response, then select Add image to upload or select an image. This will allow you to add a picture or video to the question or answer.

2. Click on Add image or Add video, respectively, to add a single image or YouTube video.

3. Click Add Section and give the new section a name to add it.

Collaboration In Google Forms

Sharing Forms with Others

Take these actions to distribute a Google Form to other people:

1. Go to Google Forms and open the form.

2. In the upper right corner of the page, click the Send button.

3. Select the way you wish to distribute your form to other people. You have three options: send an email invitation, post a link to your form on social media, or embed your form on a webpage.

4. If you decide to share a link, click Copy link to copy the URL to your form, which you can then paste to the desired location.

5. If you decide to send an email invitation, enter the recipient's email addresses and, if desired, personalize the message.

6. Should you decide to incorporate your form into a website, just copy and paste the provided HTML code into the HTML code of your website.

You can now begin gathering replies by sharing your Google Form with others.

Collecting Responses in Real-Time

To gather responses using Google Forms in real-time, take the following actions:

1. Go to Google Forms and open the form.

2. Select the tab for Responses.

3. To enable accepting responses, click the toggle button.

4. Decide how you wish to get answers. Either a brand-new spreadsheet or an already-existing one can be used to gather responses.

5. Click Create to gather answers into a new spreadsheet.

6. Click on Select existing spreadsheet and select the spreadsheet you wish to use to start collecting replies.

7. Click Create or Select to confirm your selection after you've made it.

Your form is now prepared to receive responses instantly. By selecting the Responses option, you can examine and evaluate the responses.

Advanced Features in Google Forms

Using Response Validation

Take these actions to utilize response validation in Google Forms:

1. Go to Google Forms and open the form.
2. In the upper right corner of the page, click the Settings symbol.
3. Select Quizzes.
4. Turn on the quiz feature.
5. Decide when to give pupils their grades.
6. You can decide how many tries the pupils can make.
7. Select if you want to shuffle the questions and answers.
8. Select whether to display the right answers following each question or upon quiz submission.
9. Then select Save.

By clicking on the three dots next to each question and choosing Response validation, you can now add validation criteria to your inquiries. Rules for text, numbers, and regular expressions can all be set.

Using Add-ons and Extensions

You can personalize and improve the functionality of your forms with the aid of the many add-ons and extensions that Google Forms offers. The following are a few of the most widely used extensions and add-ons:

1. Form Approvals: With this add-on, you can configure a workflow for your form responses to be approved. It is up to you to decide who must approve each response and what happens when it is approved.

2. Choice Eliminator: This add-on stops users from picking the same response more than once by removing answer alternatives from your form when they are chosen.

3. Form Publisher: With this add-on, you can use the responses to your forms to automatically create PDFs or Google Docs.

4. Form Notifications: Upon submission of a form response, this add-on notifies you and/or your team members through email.

5. Form Limiter: You can set a limit on how many responses your form can receive using this extension.

6. Quizlet: Using Quizlet flashcards, you can build quizzes with this plugin.

7. Flubaroo: With this add-on, your quizzes are automatically graded, and students receive thorough feedback.

8. Choice Redirects: Depending on the answers they select, this extension sends users to distinct web pages.

9. Form Values: You can pre-populate form fields with default values by using this extension.

10. Form Ranger: This add-on lets you use data from a Google Sheet to fill in form fields.

By clicking the three dots in the upper right corner of your Google Form and choosing Add-ons or Extensions, you can locate these add-ons and extensions.

INTEGRATIONS WITH OTHER GOOGLE WORKSPACE APPS

Using Google Forms with Google Sheets

You can build and manage surveys, quizzes, and other forms with Google Sheets and Forms, two extremely useful tools. You can use Google Sheets with Google Forms in the following ways:

1. Gathering Responses: Data from forms created in Google Forms is automatically saved in a Google Sheet. This facilitates the viewing and analysis of the information gathered from your form.

2. Data Validation: To make sure the information provided in your form is correct and comprehensive, you can use Google Sheets' data validation feature. To guarantee that only particular kinds of data are entered into particular cells, for instance, you might set up rules.

3. Data Analysis: Google Sheets offers several tools to help you analyze the information gathered from your form. Your data can be seen and analyzed with the use of pivot tables, charts, and other tools.

4. Automated Workflows: You can use add-ons such as Form Publisher to have your form responses automatically convert to PDFs or Google Docs. Additionally, you can create an approval workflow for your form responses by utilizing add-ons like Form Approvals.

5. Cooperation: You can work together on data analysis by sharing your form replies with others using Google Sheets. To collaborate on your form with others, you can also utilize comments and other tools.

6. Integration with Other Technologies: You can automate workflows across other apps by integrating Google Forms and Google Sheets with other technologies like Zapier.

CHAPTER NINE

Google Sites
INTRODUCTION

Google developed a tool called Google Sites for creating websites. It removes the requirement for technical and design expertise by enabling consumers to construct and publish websites. To build a one-of-a-kind website, Google Sites offers a selection of customizable templates and themes. Using a straightforward drag-and-drop interface, users can add text, photos, videos, and other kinds of content to their web pages. Adding files and documents to your website is simple because of Google Sites' integration with other Google Workspace applications like Google Drive.

Setting Up Google Sites
Accessing Google Sites

Take these actions to get to Google Sites:

1. Get your browser open, then navigate to sites.google.com.
2. Click on **Go to Google Sites**.
3. Open your Google account and log in.

Creating a New Site

Use these procedures to establish a new site in Google Sites:

1. Get your browser open, then navigate to sites.google.com.

2. Click on **Go to Google Sites**.

3. Open your Google account and log in.

4. To start a new website, click Create.

5. Select a template or begin building your website from scratch.

6. Use the drag-and-drop interface to add text, photos, videos, and other kinds of content to personalize your website.

7. To publish your website, click Publish.

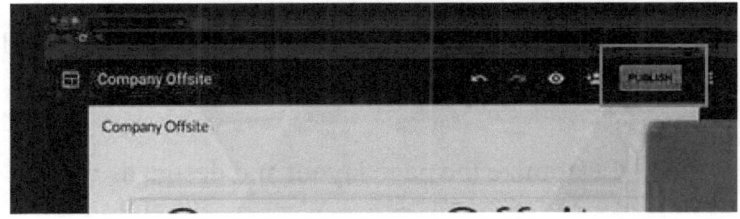

Basic Functions of Google Sites

Adding and Editing Pages

In Google Sites, to add and modify pages:

Adding a Page:

1. **Access Google Sites:** Log in to your Google account and open Google Sites (sites.google.com).

2. **Create a New Site or Open an Existing One:**

   - Click on "+ Blank" to create a new site or select an existing site.

3. **Adding a Page:**

   - On the right-hand panel, click on the "Pages" tab.

   - Click the "+" button to create a new page.

   - Give your page a name and choose its location in the site's hierarchy (parent page).

4. **Customize Page Layout:**

   - Click on "Templates" to choose a predefined layout for your page.

   - Customize the page layout and design as desired.

5. **Editing a Page:**

   - Click on the page you want to edit in the site's navigation.

   - Click the "Edit" button (pencil icon) at the top right corner of the page.

6. **Editing Content:**

   - Edit text, and add images, videos, links, or any other content using the inline editor.

   - Use the toolbar for formatting options.

7. **Adding Widgets and Gadgets:**

   - Click on "Insert" to add various elements like text boxes, images, Google Drive files, and more.

8. **Page Settings:**

   - Click on "Page settings" to adjust page-specific settings like page name, permissions, and metadata.

9. **Preview and Save:**

   - Click "Preview" to see how your page will appear to viewers.

   - Click "Save" to save your changes.

10. **Publish Changes:**

    - Click "Publish" to make your edited page live on your site.

Formatting Text:

1. Modify this page.

2. Emphasize the text.

3. Utilize the formatting toolbar.

Formatting Images:

1. Modify this page.

2. Put an image here.

3. Modify the captions, size, and placement.

4. Link to this page if necessary.

5. Save edits, then publish them.

To add a list or link, either highlight the text or click the desired location. Select the formatting option for your text from the menu at the top. While typing in a text box on Google Sites, you can change the text's size, color, font, spacing, and other attributes.

Creating Navigation Menus

To establish a hierarchy, you can add pages to your website and nest them beneath other pages. By dragging and dropping pages in the Pages area, you can easily rearrange them and nest them beneath other pages.

The navigation menu appears at the top of your website by default. If you'd like, you can reposition the navigation menu to the left, however doing so requires that your website have one or more pages. Additionally, you can decide whether to arrange your navigation vertically or horizontally.

Customizing Google Site

Theme

By choosing the Themes tab in the right sidebar and clicking the plus sign, you can start a new theme. Your theme can be altered by modifying the font style, background color, and other elements.

Adding and Customizing Site Elements

To add menus for navigation in Google Sites:

1. Modify this page.
2. Add a horizontal line.
3. Make the divider unique.
4. Add links to create a menu.
5. Organize links.
6. Save edits, then publish them.

You can customize your website with text, photos, videos, calendars, maps, and more. By changing the width of your pages and adding columns, you can further alter the way your site is laid out.

You can create and manage sites programmatically with the Google Sites API, which is useful if you want to add a custom element to your website. With the API, you can add pages, change the site's layout, and add content.

Embedding Google Drive Files and Google Maps

A Google Drive file can be embedded by opening it in Google Drive and selecting the Share option. Next, select Embed and take a copy of the HTML code that displays. Next, select Insert > Embed from your Google Site. Copy the HTML code, then click Next after it has appeared in the box. After that, click Insert after adjusting the embedded file's size.

A Google Map can be embedded by opening it in Google Maps and selecting the Share option. Next, select "Embed a map" and take a copy of the HTML code that displays. Next, select Insert > Embed from your Google Site. Copy the HTML code, then click Next after it has appeared in the box. After that, click Insert and change the embedded map's size.

COLLABORATION IN GOOGLE SITES

Sharing Sites with Others

Your site can be made public on the internet or shared with particular individuals or groups. Additionally, you control who can access, modify, and leave comments on your website.

You can click on Share in the upper right corner of your website to share it with particular individuals or groups. Next, select the permission level for each person you wish to share your site with and enter their email addresses. If desired, you can also include a message with the email invitation.

You can click on Publish in the upper right corner of your website to make it publicly accessible online. Next, decide if you want to publish a single page or your entire website. Additionally, you can decide whether to display your website in search results and to accept comments.

Advanced Features

To assist you in creating dynamic and interactive websites, Google Sites provides several sophisticated features. Here are a few of Google Sites' more sophisticated features:

1. Embed HTML, JavaScript, and CSS: To increase the functionality of your website, you can embed custom code in the form of HTML, JavaScript, or CSS. This enables you to incorporate interactive content, custom forms, and third-party widgets.
2. Custom Domains: To give your Google Site a polished and branded web address, you can map a custom domain to it using Google Workspace or a verified domain.
3. Collaborative Editing: Working on projects and websites as a team is made simple by the ability for multiple users to edit a Google Site in real time.
4. Version History: You can examine and go back to earlier iterations of Google Sites if necessary. Version history records the modifications you make to the site.
5. Advanced Layout Options: You can add more than one column, alter the page width, and change the header and footer to further personalize the layout of your website.
6. Templates: To assist you in getting started with various website types, such as project sites, event sites, and more, Google Sites provides a range of templates. Additionally, you can design your unique templates.

With Google Sites' sophisticated features, you can build highly customized, interactive websites for a range of uses, including online portfolios, project management, and marketing.

Tips And Tricks for Using Google Sites

Take into account these pointers and suggestions to make the most of Google Sites for building and maintaining websites:

1. Create a Site Structure Plan:
    *   To guarantee a clean and well-organized layout, sketch out the site's pages, content, and structure before you begin construction.

2. Employ Templates
    *   Google Sites provides templates for a range of uses. To save time and effort, start with a template that aligns with the goals of your website.

3. Personalize the Design:
    *   To present your content in the best possible way, try out various layout options, such as single-column, multiple-column, or custom layouts.

4. Incorporate Coherent Navigation:
    *   To make it easier for users to find information on your website, include a simple and easy-to-use

navigation menu. Use subpages and page headers to provide hierarchical navigation.

5. Employ subheadings and headings:

- To make your content easier to read and more accessible, use headings and subheadings. A table of contents is automatically created by Google Sites.

CHAPTER TEN

Google Chat
Introduction

Google created the communication tool known as Google Chat. Users can share files, make voice and video calls, and send and receive messages with it. Both an iOS and Android mobile app and a web version of Google Chat are accessible. Gmail, Google Meet, Google Drive, and other Google services are all integrated with it.

Setting Up Google Chat

Customizing your Chat Environment

You can improve your overall experience and customize the interface to your preferences by customizing your Google Chat environment. Here's how to alter Google Chat to your liking:

1. Profile Image:
    *   To upload a new profile picture or edit the one you already have, click on your picture in the upper right corner.
2. Standing and Intentions:
    *   To indicate your availability, set your status to that. You can select "Set status" by clicking on

your profile picture and selecting from pre-defined options such as "Available," "Away," or "Do not disturb."

3. Settings for Notifications:

   • You can customize how you receive alerts for messages and mentions by modifying your notification preferences. Right-click on your profile photo, select "Settings," then "Notifications."

4. Topics:

   • Modify the theme to give Google Chat a unique appearance. Go to "Settings," click on your profile picture, and select a theme from the "Chat theme" menu.

5. Keyboard Quick Links:

   • You can choose to enable or disable keyboard shortcuts. Press "Shift" + "?" to access keyboard shortcuts, or select "Settings" > "Keyboard shortcuts."

BASIC FUNCTIONS OF GOOGLE CHAT

Sending and Receiving Messages

In Google Chat, you can click on the + icon located in the lower-left corner of the screen and choose Message to send a message. Next, type your message in the text box that displays and enter the recipient's name or email address. You can also click on the corresponding icons to add GIFs, stickers, and emojis to your message.

You must be logged into your account and have an active internet connection to receive messages in Google Chat. If you have enabled notifications, your device will notify you when there are new messages.

Creating Group Chats

You can adhere to Google's instructions to establish a group chat in Google Chat. By clicking on the + icon in the lower-left corner of the screen and choosing Group, you can start a group chat. Next, click Create after entering the recipients' names or email addresses to join the group chat. By selecting the camera icon next to the group name, you can also upload a photo to your group chat.

Sharing Files and Links

You can adhere to Google's instructions to share files and links in Google Chat. Files from your PC, Google Drive, and other cloud storage services can all be shared. Links to other resources, such as documents and web pages, can also be shared.

You can click on the + icon in the bottom left corner of the screen and choose File to share a file from your computer. Next, choose the file from your computer that you wish to share and press Open. To share files, you can also drag and drop them into the chat window.

You can click on the + icon in the bottom left corner of the screen and choose Drive to share a file from Google Drive. Then, select the file you want to share from your Google Drive and click Insert. You can also search for files in your Google Drive by typing keywords in the search box.

To share a link to a website or document, you can copy the URL of the website or document and paste it into the chat window. You can also use the Insert Link option to add a hyperlink to your message.

Advanced Features in Google Chat

Using Chatbots to Automate Tasks

Chatbots are computer programs that can simulate conversations with human users. They can be used to automate tasks such as answering frequently asked questions, scheduling appointments, and providing customer support. Google Chat supports chatbots that can be integrated with other Google services such as Google Sheets, Google Forms, and more.

To use chatbots in Google Chat, you can follow the instructions provided by Google. You can create a chatbot using the Apps Script API or Dialogflow API. You can also use pre-built chatbots from the Google Cloud Marketplace.

Using Third-party Integrations

You can integrate with third-party apps such as Asana, Trello, Salesforce, and more. You can also create custom bots using the Apps Script API or Dialogflow API to automate tasks and workflows.

To integrate with third-party apps, you need to have the necessary permissions and credentials. You can then connect your Google Chat account to the third-party app by following the instructions provided by the app. Once connected, you can use the app's features directly within Google Chat.

COLLABORATION IN GOOGLE CHAT

Assigning Different Levels of Access

You can choose whether people can view, edit, or comment on a room. You can also add or remove members from a room and assign roles to members.

Reviewing and Analyzing Chat Activity

Reviewing and analyzing chat activity in Google Chat is important for various purposes, including monitoring communication, ensuring compliance, and improving team collaboration. Here's how you can do it:

1. **Accessing Chat History**:

   - Open Google Chat and navigate to the conversation or chat room you want to review.

2. **Message Search**:

   - Use the search bar to locate specific messages, keywords, or conversations. This is useful for quickly finding relevant information.

3. **Export Chat History**:

   - You can export chat history for archiving or analysis purposes. Click on the three dots menu in a chat, select "More," and choose "Export Chat History."

4. **Message Threads**:

   - In group chats or rooms, follow message threads to understand the context of discussions.

5. **Attachments and Files**:

   - Review attachments, files, and links shared in chats to access additional information or resources.

Tips And Tricks for Using Google Chat Efficiently

Take into account these pointers and suggestions to make effective use of Google Chat for team cooperation and communication:

1. Keyboard Quick Links:
   - Become familiar with and utilize keyboard shortcuts for frequently used tasks including text formatting, chat navigation, and message composition. To view the available shortcuts, press "Shift" + "?"

2. Labels and Stars:

- Mark significant discussions or messages so you can find them quickly afterward. Labels can also be used to classify and arrange discussions.

3. Notifications and Mentions:
   - In a conversation, use "@mentions" to get someone's attention. Adapt your notification preferences to minimize distractions and ensure you never miss an essential communication.

4. Functionality of Search:
   - Use the search box to swiftly locate particular conversations, files, or messages. Search results can be filtered based on sender, category, or date.

5. Chat Threads:
   - Respond inside message threads to keep discussions tidy. This clears up confusion and facilitates following conversations.

CHAPTER ELEVEN

Admin Console
INTRODUCTION TO THE ADMIN CONSOLE

What is the Admin Console?

Google Workspace services can be managed by administrators using a web-based interface called the Google Admin Console. It offers a single area where users, groups, devices, and services can all be managed. The Admin Console allows administrators to do a variety of tasks, including setting up security rules, configuring settings for Google Drive and Gmail, and creating and managing user accounts.

How to Access the Admin Console

To access the admin console:

1. Visit the login page.

2. Enter admin credentials.

3. Navigate to admin controls.

4. Complete tasks as needed.

5. Log out securely.

You can use your administrator account to log into the Admin Console. If you lack an administrator account, you can make one by following Google's guidelines.

Overview of the Admin Console Interface

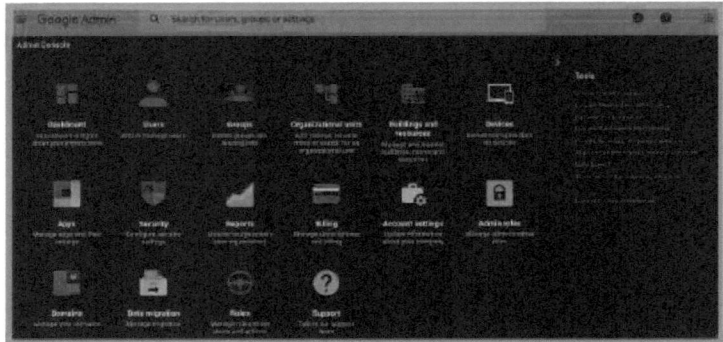

Admin Roles

The various admin roles offered by Google Workspace define the degree of authority and control an administrator has over the Google Workspace services used by the company. Among the open admin jobs are:

1. Super Admin: Capable of overseeing every facet of the company's Google Workspace account and having access to all services.
2. Admin of Groups: Able to control groups and group configurations.

3. Password resets, user information management, and account creation and management are all possible with the User Management Admin.

4. Help Desk Administrator: Able to reset passwords and offer assistance to users.

5. Gmail, Google Drive, and other Google Workspace services can be managed by a service administrator.

Users in your company can be given admin roles by following Google's recommendations.

Apps

You can administer the Google Workspace services for your company by using several applications that are accessible through the Admin Console. Among these applications are:

1. Emails can be sent and received using Gmail, a web-based email service.

2. Google Drive: A cloud storage platform that facilitates content sharing and storing for users.

3. One online word-processing tool that lets users generate and modify documents is Google Docs.

4. Spreadsheets can be created and edited online with Google Sheets, an application for spreadsheets.

5. Creating and editing presentations is possible with Google Slides, an online presentation tool.

6. A web-based tool called Google Forms lets users make and distribute quizzes and surveys.

7. Google Sites: An online platform for building and publishing websites that everyone can use.

Billing

You can control payments and invoices for your Google Workspace services through the Admin Console. You have access to adjust your membership, change your payment method, and see your billing history. To get alerts when your account balance crosses a specific threshold, you can also set up billing alerts.

To get help with any billing-related queries or problems with the Admin Console, get in touch with Google Workspace support.

Account Settings

You can control several account settings, including user data and security configurations, through the Admin Console. Additionally, you have control over your Google Workspace service billing and payments.

For help with any queries or problems you can be experiencing with account settings in the Admin Console, get in touch with Google Workspace support.

Data Migration

Data from many email platforms, including IBM Notes, Microsoft Exchange, and others, can be migrated. Additionally, data from other cloud storage services like Dropbox, Box, and others can be migrated.

To get help with any queries or problems with data transfer in Google Workspace, get in touch with Google Workspace support.

Devices

The efficient administration of devices is an essential component of contemporary organizational operations. Businesses and organizations in today's digital environment depend on a wide range of devices to support work, communication, and productivity. Computers, cellphones, tablets, and even Internet of Things (IoT) devices are among these gadgets. Ensuring data protection, compliance, and operational continuity requires effective and secure management of these devices.

Security

Any firm must prioritize security, and the Admin Console provides powerful tools to strengthen it. In addition to managing device access and enabling multi-factor authentication, administrators can enforce security standards. Through the Security Center, the console also offers administrators insights on security risks, enabling them to remain attentive and take preventative action to safeguard the data of their firm.

Reports

With the console's extensive reporting features, managers can keep tabs on user behavior, observe use patterns, and provide reports on a range of Google Workspace usage topics for their company. Both resource optimization and the detection of security risks can benefit from this knowledge.

Users

Admins can designate organizational units, add, edit, or remove user accounts, and manage which Google services users can access. To improve security, they might also impose strict password regulations and change passwords.

Navigating the Google Admin Console

The Google Admin Console must be navigated to manage the several services and settings related to Google Workspace (previously G Suite) for your company. This is the way to use the Google Admin Console:

1. **Sign In:**

   - Go to the Google Admin Console login page (admin.google.com).

   - Sign in with your administrator account credentials.

2. **Dashboard:**

   - After signing in, you will land on the Admin Console dashboard.

   - The dashboard provides an overview of your organization's Google Workspace services, user activity, and important announcements.

3. **Navigation Menu:**

   - On the left side of the dashboard, you'll find the navigation menu.

- This menu allows you to access various sections and settings within the Admin Console.

4. **Main Sections:**

- The Admin Console is organized into several main sections, including but not limited to:

  - **Users:** Manage user accounts, groups, and organizational units.

  - **Apps:** Control and configure Google Workspace applications.

  - **Device Management:** Enroll and manage mobile devices and Chrome devices.

  - **Security:** Configure security settings and manage security alerts.

  - **Billing:** Handle billing and payment information.

  - **Reports:** Access usage reports and audit logs.

  - **Settings:** Configure general settings for your organization.

User Management in The Admin Console

Adding and Removing Users

Managing user accounts and access rights in different software programs or systems, such as email services, cloud platforms, or content management systems, is sometimes referred to as adding and deleting users in an admin panel. Though the exact processes can differ based on the system you're using, I can give you a rough rundown of how it works.

Adding Users in Admin Console:

1. Access the Admin interface: To add users, log in to the application's or system's admin interface. Administrator rights might be required to use this console.

2. Navigate to User Management: In the admin interface, look for a user management-related section or menu. You can see this section titled "Account Management," "Users," "User Management," or a similar term.

3. Include a New User:

    a. Click on the option to add a new user or create a new account.

b. Fill in the required user information, which typically includes:

    i. User's full name

    ii. Email address

    iii. Username (if applicable)

    iv. Password (or a way to set up a password)

    v. User role or permissions (e.g., admin, regular user, etc.)

c. Depending on the system, you can also need to set additional user attributes or configure specific settings.

4. Examine and Verify: Verify that the data you submitted is accurate by checking it again. Next, verify that the new user account has been created.

5. Notify the User: If required, let the new user know that their account has been created, give them their login credentials, and provide them with any other pertinent information.

Removing Users in Admin Console:

1. **Access the Admin Console:** Log in to the admin console of the application or system where you want to remove users.

2. **Navigate to User Management:** Locate the section or menu related to user management, as mentioned in the previous steps.

3. **Find the User to Remove:**

   - Search for the user you want to remove by their name, email address, or username.

   - Select the user account to access its details.

4. **Remove the User:**

   - Look for an option like "Delete," "Remove," or "Deactivate" to remove the user.

   - Confirm the action when prompted. Depending on the system, you can be asked to confirm by entering your admin credentials or providing a reason for the removal.

5. **Notify the User (Optional):** If it's appropriate and necessary, inform the user that their account has been removed.

6. **Review and Cleanup (Optional):** After removing a user, consider reviewing their access permissions, shared data, and any other resources associated with their account. You can need to reassign or manage these resources accordingly.

Update a User's Name or Email

In an admin console, to change a user's email address or name:

1. Log in to the admin console.

2. Navigate to User Management or User Settings.

3. Find the user whose name or email you want to update.

4. Select the user's profile.

5. Edit the user's name or email.

6. Save or confirm the changes.

Filtering Users

Utilizing an admin panel to filter users:

1. Open the admin console and log in.

2. Navigate to the User List or User Management area.

3. Seek out choices for sorting or filtering (such as the search bar, filters, or sorting).
4. Use criteria such as username, role, status, or other properties to apply filters.
5. Examine the list of users who have been filtered to match your criteria.

Create an Alternate Email Address or Alias

To set up a user's alias or backup email address in an admin console:

1. Open the admin console and log in.
2. Go to User Settings or User Management.
3. Locate the user that you wish to set up an alias for.
4. Choose the profile of the user.
5. Search for a feature that has to do with email aliases or different email addresses.
6. Incorporate the preferred pseudonym or different email address.
7. Verify or save the modifications.

Device Management in The Admin Console

Enrolling and Managing Devices

To use an admin console to enroll and manage devices:

1. Access the device management platform or system by logging into the admin console.
2. Go to the enrollment or device management area.
3. Activate a New Device:
   - Add a new device by providing its information, such as the device type, user, and device identifier (such as the IMEI or serial number).
   - Adjust the permissions and settings on your device as necessary.
4. Control Devices:
   - See the list of devices that are enrolled.
   - Adjust permissions, policies, or device settings.
   - Monitor use and device status.
   - Take actions such as remote troubleshooting, erasing, and locking.
5. Observe and Protect:
   - Keep an eye on device security and compliance.
   - Should it be required, put security measures like encryption and remote wipes into place.
   - Verify that software and security fixes are installed on devices.

6. Disable or Unenroll Devices:

- Unenroll or remove devices from management as needed.

- If necessary, securely remove data from unenrolled devices.

Managing Device Settings and Policies

To use an admin console to control device settings and policies:

1. Access the device management platform or system by logging into the admin console.

2. Go to the device settings and policies area.

3. Establish or Adjust Policies:

- Draft new policies or amend current ones. Application limitations, access controls, and security settings are a few examples of these policies.

4. Implement Device Policies:

- Choose which devices, or groups of devices, to apply the policies to.

- Assign the policies to the selected groups or devices.

5. Set up the Device's Settings:

- Reconfigure email accounts, device limitations, and Wi-Fi setups, among other device-specific options.
- Adjust the parameters to meet the needs of your company.

CHAPTER TWELVE

Security And Compliance

Introduction

Strong security and compliance features are included in Google Workspace, and they include:

1. Data encryption: Both in-transit and at-rest data are encrypted.
2. Identity and Access Management: Administrators can apply multi-factor authentication and restrict user access.
3. Manage and secure the devices that access Google Workspace using endpoint management.
4. Data Loss Prevention (DLP): Use rules based on policies to stop data leaks.
5. Audit and Reporting: Comprehensive audit records and reporting to ensure adherence to regulations.
6. Identification of Security concerns: Recognize and address security concerns.
7. Certifications for Compliance: Google Workspace complies with several industry standards.
8. Legal and compliance teams can search and export data using eDiscovery tools.
9. Retention and Archiving: Establish guidelines for data retention and archiving.

10. Security Center: a centralized information and control center for security.

SECURING YOUR GOOGLE WORKSPACE ACCOUNT

Setting Up Two-Factor Authentication

To set up Two-Factor Authentication (2FA) in Google Workspace:

1. **Admin Console**: Sign in as an admin.

2. **Security**: Navigate to "Security" in the Admin Console.

3. **Basic Settings**: Under "Basic settings," enable "2-Step Verification."

4. **Enroll Users**: Enroll users in 2FA through the Admin Console or instruct them to set it up individually.

5. **Verification Methods**: Users can choose from methods like text, call, or Google Authenticator.

6. **Backup Codes**: Encourage users to generate and save backup codes.

7. **Security Keys**: Consider using hardware security keys for added security.

8. **Enforcement**: Optionally, enforce 2FA for all users.

2FA enhances the security of Google Workspace accounts by requiring an additional verification step beyond a password.

Creating strong passwords:

1. **Length**: Use at least 12 characters.

2. **Complexity**: Include a mix of uppercase, lowercase, numbers, and symbols.

3. **Avoid Common Words**: Don't use easily guessable words or phrases.

4. **Unpredictability**: Avoid predictable patterns or keyboard sequences.

5. **Unique for Each Account**: Use different passwords for different accounts.

6. **Passphrases**: Consider using random phrases or acronyms for added length.

7. **Password Managers**: Use a reputable password manager to generate and store complex passwords securely.

8. **Change Regularly**: Periodically change passwords, especially for critical accounts.

9. **Two-Factor Authentication (2FA)**: Enable 2FA whenever possible for an extra layer of security.

10. **Avoid Personal Information**: Don't use easily discoverable personal information, like birthdays or names.

Strong passwords help protect your accounts from unauthorized access.

Auditing And Monitoring Activity In Google Workspace

Best Practices For Security And Compliance In Google Workspace

Regularly Reviewing and Updating Security Policies To ensure that your company's security procedures continue to be successful, you must regularly evaluate and update Google Workspace security rules. Here's how this procedure is explained:

1. Continuous Improvement: Over time, best practices and security threats change. Your security policies

will remain up-to-date and effective against emerging threats if they are regularly reviewed.

2. Compliance: Requirements for compliance might alter. Keeping your policies current will assist in guaranteeing that your company continues to adhere to industry norms and requirements.

3. Features: Google Workspace regularly releases updates with additional settings and security features. You can improve your security posture by using these features regularly with reviews.

4. User Education: User behavior frequently affects security policy. Periodic evaluations offer chances to reaffirm users' understanding of security and inform them of new regulations.

5. Revision of policies aids in the improvement of incident response plans and protocols, guaranteeing that your company is capable of handling security issues with efficiency.

6. Risk assessment: You can modify policies in response to emerging threats or changes in the threat landscape by conducting ongoing risk assessments.

7. Integration of input: To improve the protection and usability of policies, collect and analyze input from security incidents and user experiences.

8. Policy Documentation: Keep policy documentation up to date to facilitate understanding and adherence to security rules by administrators and users alike.

9. Testing and Simulation: To evaluate security policies and pinpoint areas for improvement, test them regularly using drills or simulations.

Providing Security Awareness Training to Employees

For several reasons, educating staff members about security awareness is an essential auditing and monitoring task in Google Workspace.

1. User Behavior: It aids in evaluating how well staff members comprehend and follow organizational security rules and procedures.

2. Compliance: Consistent security training guarantees that staff members understand and abide by security norms and rules, which is frequently necessary in several businesses.

3. Phishing Awareness: Employees' capacity to identify and react to phishing efforts, a prevalent security risk, can be evaluated by tracking the efficacy of training.

4. Data handling: It evaluates workers' familiarity with secure data handling, which is essential for safeguarding private data.

Security Assessments and Vulnerability Testing

To detect and reduce possible security threats in Google Workspace, security assessments and vulnerability testing are essential. Here is the justification:

1. Finding Weaknesses: Security evaluations and vulnerability testing entail a methodical inspection of Google Workspace apps, infrastructure, and configurations to find potential vulnerabilities, misconfigurations, and weaknesses.

2. Risk Mitigation: You can lessen the possibility of security incidents or breaches by taking proactive measures to discover vulnerabilities and weaknesses early on.

3. Compliance: Consistent evaluations assist in guaranteeing that your company continues to adhere to security guidelines, rules, and best practices.

4. Patch Management: By identifying out-of-date software or systems that require patching, vulnerability testing

enables you to keep your environment up to date with security updates.

CHAPTER THIRTEEN

Monetization And Productivity Tips

REVENUE POTENTIAL WITH GOOGLE WORKSPACE

The potential income from Google Workspace is contingent upon several aspects, including the organization's size and nature, the degree of customization and support needed, and the selected price plan. Google Workspace provides chances for both direct and indirect income generation.

1. Subscription Fees: The main source of income for Google Workspace is subscription fees. Businesses pay a monthly fee per user to use the range of collaboration and productivity tools. The number of users determines how much money can be made.

2. Business and Enterprise editions of Workspace are among the several variants that Google provides. With its extensive security and compliance capabilities, the Enterprise edition usually commands a higher subscription price, which might result in more income for Google.

3. Extra Services: Google Workspace can be combined with extra services like Chrome Enterprise or Google

Cloud Platform (GCP), which increases income for Google through cross-selling.

4. Authorized reseller partners are permitted by Google to market and provide support for Google Workspace. By offering firms advice, integration, migration, and support services, these partners generate income.

5. Third-Party Apps: Through the Google Workspace Marketplace, third-party developers can earn money by creating and offering connectors and add-on apps for Google Workspace.

Tips For Boosting Your Productivity In Google Workspace

Think about the following advice to increase your productivity in Google Workspace:

1. Use Keyboard Shortcuts: To browse and do activities more quickly, become familiar with the keyboard shortcuts for Gmail, Google Docs, and other Google Workspace apps.

2. Organize Your Inbox: To keep your email organized and less cluttered, use Gmail's labels, filters, and priority inbox features.

3. Templates: To save time on repeated chores, create templates for documents or emails that you use regularly.

4. Google Drive Organization: To make it easier to locate and manage your work, keep your Google Drive organized with folders and distinct file names.

5. Google Calendar Scheduling: Make effective use of Google Calendar's scheduling tools, such as calendar sharing and reminder settings, to arrange meetings and appointments.

6. Google Keep: For task lists and rapid note-taking, use Google Keep. Easily productive, it combines with other Google apps.

7. Collaborative Editing: For effective cooperation, take advantage of real-time collaboration in Google Sheets, Slides, and Docs.

8. Google Forms: Create and utilize Google Forms to collect data, conduct surveys, and get feedback.

Templates, macros, and automation are a few examples of tools and methods that might help you work more efficiently and quickly.

You can work more quickly and intelligently by using the following tools and techniques:

1. Templates: Pre-made formats for documents, emails, and presentations help to save time while creating and

formatting information. Gmail's email templates and Google Docs' document templates are two examples.

2. Macros: In programs like Microsoft Excel or Google Sheets, macros are scripts or recorded actions that automate repetitive activities. They can complete tasks like sorting, formatting, and computations swiftly.

3. Automation Tools: By integrating many apps and initiating activities based on predetermined criteria, tools like Zapier and Integromat automate workflows.

4. Text Expansion: By creating shortcuts for often-used words, you can avoid entering them repeatedly by using text expansion tools like TextExpander.

5. Software for managing tasks and projects: Programs like Trello, Asana, or Google Tasks assist you in setting priorities and organizing work, which boosts output and teamwork.

Tips for Troubleshooting Common Issues in Google Workspace

Here are some pointers for resolving typical problems with Google Workspace:

1. Check Service Status: Go to the Google Workspace Status Dashboard to find out whether your problem is

being caused by any known service outages or interruptions.

2. Empty Browser Cache: Try emptying the cache and cookies in your browser if you're having problems using Google Workspace applications in your browser.

3. Browser Compatibility: To get the most out of Google Workspace, make sure your web browser is supported and up to current.

4. Check Internet Connection: Google Workspace functionality can be impacted by unstable or improperly functioning internet connections. Therefore, make sure these are stable and operational.

5. Device Reboots: Occasionally, problems with an app's performance or connectivity can be fixed with a quick restart of your computer or mobile device.

6. Disable Browser Extensions: Google Workspace can occasionally be interfered with by browser add-ons or extensions. Disable them for a short while to see if it solves the issue.

7. Update Apps: Make sure that all of your Google Workspace applications, including Google Drive and Gmail, are current. Older applications can have compatibility problems or bugs.

Making Google Workspace More Accessible for People with Disabilities

To guarantee that everyone can utilize Google Workspace's capabilities to the fullest, it is imperative to make the platform more accessible to those with impairments. The following actions can improve accessibility:

1. **Enable Accessibility Features**:

    - In Google Workspace apps, go to "Settings" or "Preferences" and enable accessibility features such as screen readers, voice commands, and keyboard shortcuts.

2. **Keyboard Navigation**:

    - Ensure that all Google Workspace apps are navigable and usable via keyboard commands for individuals who cannot use a mouse.

3. **Screen Reader Support**:

    - Google Workspace apps, like Google Docs and Gmail, work with popular screen readers like JAWS, NVDA, and Voiceover. Ensure these features are enabled and optimized for compatibility.

4. **High-Contrast Themes**:

- Use high-contrast themes or dark modes in Google Workspace apps to make content more readable for users with low vision or visual impairments.

5. **Alt Text for Images**:

   - Add meaningful alternative text (alt text) to images and graphics to provide context for screen readers.

6. **Keyboard Shortcuts and Voice Commands**:

   - Promote awareness of keyboard shortcuts and voice command functionality, as they can greatly improve accessibility.

Made in United States
Troutdale, OR
03/05/2024

18230569R00096